9 Moons of Hekate
Herbalism of Hekate

Copyright © 2022 Jennifer Teixeira

First paperback edition October 2022

ISBN 979-8-9855266-3-9 (Paperback)
ISBN 979-8-9855266-1-5
(Hardcover)

"Radical Magical Hekate" Paperback cover art
by Metzalli Quetzal Guel Van Dyne High
Priestess and Artist Living in Santa Fe

9 Moons of Hekate

By Jennifer Teixeira

Many Thanks to Danica, Yemaya, Pennyroyal, Iris, Laura, The Eureka Grove of Hekate, Quetzal, Ash, Jack, Yansumi, Akasha, Rowan, Jenny, Manea, Heaven, Laurie, Heather, Ariel, my Mother, my Father, to all those who read this book, and the Mighty Queen Herself.

"The Goddess Hekate taught to handle magic herbs with exceeding skill all that the land and flowing waters produce" *Argonautica*

How can a simple book tell you how to work with this mighty and multi-faceted Goddess? In reality,, it cannot. This book gives you an idea of how to work with her. The Goddess Hekate has many forms, many different ways to perceive. She is a goddess of Change and Transition, she who manifests at the crossroads of life, death and rebirth is not stagnant as her path is that of the flow of existence.

This book will guide you through the world of herbs, the basics of modern herbalism and how to work with them in relation to the Goddess Hekate.

Hekate is a Goddess that has been worshiped for thousands of years. She is mentioned in the Greek Magical Papyri as a worker of magic for the benefit of the clientele of professional Sorcerer(s) in Roman ruled Egypt, and in the Chaldean Oracles as the Cosmic World Soul, the one who ignites the spark of life in this body of flesh. She also appears in Hesiod's Theogony as ruler of Heaven, Earth and Sea, in Homer's Odyssey and The Hymn to Demeter, and in portions of texts by Sophocles like The Root Cutters. Hekate has been called "The Persian Queen," which some will say means she is the daughter of Perses, though it is also said that her origins come from Thrace which was ruled by Persians for a time, there is some debate as to whether or not she may have originally been from Sumeria. The Sumerian Goddess Gula had similar attributes to Hekate as she was known to be a Goddess associated with Dogs. Dogs were seen to have healing powers in the way they would lick their wounds and each other, they would eat grass to purge, and also offered their protection. Gula was a Goddess of healing, protection and patroness to herbalists. Hekate's Epiphany to this day is the Black dog. The barking of dogs is a sign she is near, and if you see one of her hounds, it is most certainly a sign that your magic is drawing her attention. The evolution of Hekate throughout the centuries teaches us much, her multifaceted nature has inspired many people to gather at her temples, as her fires lead the way.

Herbalism has its own language, terms and descriptors for methods of extracting. This is a short guide to these methods and terms to give you an idea on different ways of preparation. As said in the Introduction, much of the methods of preparation have been written down in great detail by our own predecessors. Some of which will be listed in the references section if you wish to dive deeper. The following is our current language for these processes, this can make finding more information on them easier as now we can do a simple search on the internet or ask questions of people with more experience than us. You may have been doing some or all of these things already, for hundreds if not thousands of years this work was learned by observing another doing it, and it was passed on this way. Now we can learn from books, but you may already have some of this written in your DNA and do it subconsciously.

You will notice that one plant may have many different names, things like "Eye of Newt " were code names. The Eye of Newt is actually Mustard Seed. Lion's Foot is the herb Lady's Mantle. You may find that one herb will have many given names, so it is best to go by scientific names if you are purchasing herbs at the market. This will help you to maintain consistency in your recipes. When you purchase herbs from the market, be sure you are buying from reputable and ethical sources. As a side note, you can do your own blessing charm for the spirit of the herbs even if they have been dried.

Some herbs will be better harvested at certain times of the year, and even parts of the plant will have more potency in the 2nd or 3rd year of their growth. For example, you will not see mullein flowers until the plant is in its second year. The potency of Dream root is best in its 2nd year as well. Depending on where you are located you may see plants emerging in late winter instead of early spring, or flowers forming at the beginning of summer as opposed to late spring. I encourage you to observe the plant life around you and note the changes you see in your journal for each season. You should be meeting plants on their timeline, not on what you perceive their timeline should be. If you read in one book that you should harvest this particular root at a certain time, that may well be true, but still observe your environment and listen to what the plants say.

Keep in mind roots are generally harvested when the plant energy is focused on the root and growing in the earth. This can be observed when the top portion of the plant begins to brown. This will tell you the plant is done for the season, it is its way of speaking to you. One can feel the energy of the plant by sitting in meditation with it, thinking about its planetary correspondences, growth habits and/or medicinal and spiritual applications. Obviously if you are using the flowers or seed, it is when they come up and you have them available to you. There may be leaves of a different color that are useful at different times of year. Ginkgo is an example of a tree that will have different uses if the color of the leaves are green vs. gold. Keep in mind the fact that a plant's characteristics will vary depending on location. That a species may have stunted growth if it is grown in rocky soil versus a softer aerated one, or a plant may reach for the sun if it is growing in a place untouched by light. These are all things to observe, as a plant can look very different depending on all of the factors in its environment. Acknowledging a plant's strengths in relationship to its environment (what is its preferred environment?) is something you should be writing about in your personal plant journal, and this is something that will provide more data as the seasons and years go on.

The following terms are commonly found in herbalism and many of them have been mentioned in this book. Here are some of the definitions.

Herbalism Basics

What is a Solvent? When you wish to extract chemical constituents of plants, you will need some kind of solvent. This process sounds more complicated than it is. Water is the most common solvent and is used to brew tea. Other solvents include ; alcohol, vegetable glycerine, vinegar, wine, milk, honey and some kind of fat like vegetable oil or animal fat. Different solvents will extract certain constituents from their individual plants. Alcohol generally extracts more of the active constituents than vegetable glycerine, but not everyone is OK with the energetics of alcohol. Finding the best solvent for each work is part of the process.

Infusion: This is typically done by pouring 8 ounces of hot water over one tablespoon of herbal tea and letting it steep for 10-20 minutes. Infusions are used for aerial parts of herbs, leaves, and flowers. It should be noted that black, green, red and white teas are infused for no longer than 5 minutes, unless you enjoy a more astringent brew.

Decoction: Simmering roots, and heavier more dense portions of the plants is called a decoction. Typically the root or bark is simmered for 20 minutes on low heat, covered. This allows for optimum extraction. Certain mushrooms will need to simmer for a lot longer than that to break down the cell wall to be digestible. The recommended amount of herbs per 8 ounce cup of tea is typically 1 teaspoon. In some cases simmering will degrade certain compounds in your plant material, take psilocybin mushroom for example, boiling this mushroom (overheating) will destroy some of its desired active ingredients.

Cold Infusion: No heat is applied, it is simply extracted by the water overnight. Cold infusion is recommended when one wishes to extract more of the mucilaginous polysaccharides in a plant. (marshmallow root is the most used example) To do a cold infusion you simply add two tablespoons of herb to 12 ounces of water in a jar and let it extract for 6 hours or more.

Moon Infusion: A cold infusion can be adapted to gather the energy of the full moon by placing the herbs and water in a clear glass jar overnight, and allowing moonlight to come through the jar. You can put the lid on the jar to prevent any dust or insects from gaining access to the tea. This is helpful when you want to imbibe lunar energy. Lunar energy is useful for increasing powers of divination and working with dreams. This can also be adapted to make lunar oils and other items.

Solar infusion: A solar infusion is basically a cold infusion, but will be warmed by the light of the sun. Place your jar of water and herbs into a jar left in the sun's light for as many hours as the sun is up, from dawn till dusk. This will help imbue solar energy into your infusion. Solar energy is youthful, energetic and prosperous.

Flower Essence: The essence of a plant is captured in water and preserved with alcohol or vegetable glycerine. There are many ways to create a flower essence, some will gather the early morning dew from a plant and just a few drops mixed with spring water can imbue the elixir with the energetic qualities of that plant. Another method is placing the receptacle of water next to the plant or portion of the plant you are working with. And yet another method is to create a mandala of flower petals around your receptacle of water and offer your prayers and wishes from the plant energy you are working with. The focus is not using a solvent at all, it is simply imbibing your brew with the soul essence of the plant or the energy of a place and time.

Tinctures: Sometimes you will find that people will use the word "tincture" to universally mean a herb that has been extracted with any liquid. But these are preparations with alcohol being your solvent. The alcohol will help extract the plant constituents and to help preserve the herbal medicine for long term use and storage. Typical instructions for strength of alcohol will depend on what portion of a plant is being used in the tincture. Roots and heavier parts like bark will need a high proof (at least 120 proof) ethanol, aguardente or everclear. Lighter parts of the plant can use 80-100 proof alcohol. The herb material is left to infuse in the alcohol solvent for a full moon cycle. Then it is strained of its bulk material or "marc " and the liquid is decanted into its own dropper bottle for later use. The marc can be dehydrated for use in teas if desired. Fresh or dry herbs can be used depending on what works better for each individual plant.

Oil Extract: This is an oil extract that can be taken internally and/or used topically. The plant material is simmered with plant oil or animal fat as the solvent on low heat for hours. If you have time the oil and herb can be infused for a full moon cycle (from full moon to full moon/30 days approx) . Most commonly used oils are MCT, Coconut, olive and grapeseed. This can be taken by the spoonful if solid oil is used or by the dropperful if it is liquid at room temperature. Also the oil extract can be used topically or made into a salve.

Glycerites: Made using glycerine that typically comes from coconut, palm or soy. Glycerites are similar to tinctures in that they are used to preserve herbal material for later use. Glycerites have a shorter shelf life but are more suitable for children and people who choose to avoid alcohol. To make a glycerite you would use half the volume of liquid glycerine to half distilled water and extract your leafy herbs with that 1/2 and 1/2 mixture. Glycerine is a sweet syrupy substance and is palatable to many people. Glycerine will not work for every herb and sometimes it is mixed with alcohol to better extract, preserve and flavor the final product. (sort of defeats the purpose if you are trying to avoid alcohol, it just makes the concoction sweet)

Infused Vinegar: Raw apple cider vinegar is a favorite vinegar to extract the flavors, medicinal and magical properties of herbs. You can use any vinegar for this preparation, though some vinegars will be more acidic than others. The process involves pouring vinegar over your herbs, fruits, etc, and allowing them to take on the flavors, medicinal and magical properties of the plants themselves over time.

Infused Honey: Fresh herbs and roots are chopped then placed in a jar and honey poured over and left to extract for a month or more. Since the herbs are fresh, there is a chance that the herbs will mold if they are exposed to the air, be sure to have the herbal roughage covered completely. Strain out the herbs and use in tea if appropriate. You can use a cheesecloth, nut bag or stainless steel strainer to separate the bulk material from the infused honey.

Alcohol Intermediary Method can be used to prevent spoilage. Place all the herbs in the jar, and add ¼ of a teaspoon of Ethanol to the herbs in the jar, cover and shake the alcohol so that it coats all the herbs, then leave the herb jar open overnight, so most of the alcohol can evaporate. Then add your honey or oil the next day. This gives your preparation an added layer of extraction and another layer of preservation. (Works well with oils or fats to make salve.)

Oxymel: Oxymel is a preparation that is a mixture of herbally infused honey and herbally infused vinegar. The oxymel can be taken as a daily tonic or as needed depending on what the purpose of it is. Oxymel simply translates to acid and honey, Oxymels are always made with honey but there are other popular ways to make similar healthful beverages without honey; switchels and shrubs are popular at bars and health food shops and they may use other sweeteners like sugar, molasses and/or agave nectar.

Syrups: Sweetening and drawing spells will often require what resembles a syrup. To make your own syrup is very simple, but there are many ways to do it. The easiest in my opinion is to make a strong tincture with brandy (or other high proof alcohol) and once the tincture is fully extracted you can strain out the bulk herb material (also called the Marc) then you can add an equal amount of honey to the tincture, mix well and you can use this magically and medicinally. This type of syrup will have a long shelf life due to the honey and brandy combo. Another way is to create a strong infusion or decoction first with fruit, herbs or roots, then once you have strained the herbs from the water, you will add an equal amount of white sugar, and simmer till it is thick. You will need to keep it at low heat to thicken the syrup and this can take a couple of hours. Sugar does have some ability to preserve, but with the amount of water used, I would keep this refrigerated and use it within two weeks. Adding 20 percent ethanol will offer some additional preservation.

Salve: Infused oils are oftentimes made into salve using beeswax, fat and or cocoa butter. These balms can be perfumed with melted resins, floral waxes and/or sap to infuse it with a particular energy. Flying Ointments are an example of these salves or balms being used for magical purposes, to help gain spirit flight and guide a practitioner to the Witches Sabbat. A Salve can also help heal skin, and keep the skin moist to prevent further damage. Some of the simplest salves can be imbued with healing energy or even a touch of Venusian glamor magic. Here is a example of a salve made with a mysterious "Titan Root" (Mandrake)
Apollonius Rhodius, Argonautica 3. 840 ff :

"Medea wished to drive to the splendid Temple of Hekate; and while the handmaidens were getting the carriage ready she took a magic ointment from her box. This salve was named after Prometheus. A man had only to smear it on his body, after propitiating the only-begotten Maiden (*Koure mounogenes*) [Hekate] with a midnight offering, to become invulnerable by sword or fire and for that day to surpass himself in strength and daring. It first appeared in a plant that sprang from the blood-like ichor of Prometheus in his torment, which the flesh-eating eagle had dropped on the spurs of Kaukasos (Caucasus) . . . To make the ointment, Medea, clothed in black, in the gloom of night, had drawn off this juice in a Caspian shell after bathing in seven perennial streams and calling seven times on Brimo [Hekate], nurse of youth (*kourotrophos*), Brimo, night-wanderer of the underworld (*nyktipolis khthonie*), Queen of the dead (*anassa eneroi*). The dark earth shook and rumbled underneath the Titan root when it was cut, and Prometheus himself groaned in the anguish of his soul."

Poultice: A poultice is made using ground up herbs that are placed on the skin, meant to help heal or draw out. There are several different ways to make a poultice. Here are two of my favorite ways. Take fresh herbs and blend using a blender, mix 50% herbs with 50% water, strain out the bulk herb material (or Marc) and apply that to the area of the body that needs it, wrap it in muslin or plastic wrap for the appropriate amount of time. If the herb is something you can consume, then the herbal water can be taken by mouth for its healing properties, or it can be given back to the plant. Another way to make a poultice is to chop the leaves (fresh is better, but dry will work) and simmer them on low heat for 10 minutes, then strain the roughage and apply to the area when it has cooled just enough but is still warm (sometimes called a fomentation). Place in the muslin cloth and on the skin. (muslin cloth that has been moistened in the liquid of the herb being used.) This hot method is sometimes called a fomentation.

As you can see there is the option of using something that is cold, and something that is hot. Remember that cold will constrict blood vessels (Suitable for right after injury to prevent swelling) and a warm option that will allow for circulation and blood flow to the area in question. Some herbalists will alternate between the two for better circulation The choice on what to use is up to your discretion.

Mud pack: Clay gathered from various parts of the world can be mixed with powdered and dried herbs. Typically you see these herbs used to invoke beauty or to draw out infections, venom or foreign objects (splinters, stingers, etc). Red clay is more of a medicinal clay useful for drawing out and Kaolin clay is a gentle clay most often used in beauty care to tighten and invigorate skin.

The Self

It is important to note that here, in this book, you take your own life and story into your hands. You will be going on a journey to the realms of Hekate from this point forward. My suggestion is to read through the book in its entirety, then do the work. This way you have a better idea of the work involved, the items to procure and the dedication you must have for the next 9 months.

This book was intended to be an outline for initiation into the mysteries of Hekate and her realm of plants. This is simply the beginning of becoming one of her aspiring dedicants, living your life guided by her mysteries and taking your first steps into the earthly realm of plants and magic.

Know from this point forward you must use your own best judgement, you must be educating yourself along the way. If you do not understand something in this book, then you must find out more information on it. This is part of the journey, as a book cannot make you feel or understand, you must actively engage with the outside world of nature to gain this knowledge.

Self-awareness is important when you work in the realm of plants. Be someone they can see clearly by having boundaries, ethics and patience radiating from the inside out. Since you have chosen to walk this path, you are in control of it. The only person who can decide how you approach this work is you, however you will receive guidance on how to determine what your own set of ethics will look like. How you determine what is right and wrong will help guide your work, and you must make sure your goals lineup with your ethics. If they do not, ethics can feel like a wall that is put in front of you like a road block.

Think about whether the plant material you use is obtained in unethical ways, without thought and foresight into what may happen after the work is done. Imagine you begin to plant Poison Hemlock in your backyard, maybe it is in a pot or small area. You are planning to work with the plant energetically and maybe to do more research into it as a magical ingredient. Poison Hemlock is an invasive plant, one that is incredibly hard to eradicate once established in an area. The seeds will spread, and even if you think you've uprooted the plant, it can come back. It is also very poisonous and consuming only a few of the leaves can kill a person. It is likely that this plant already grows near you on a roadside or near a body of freshwater. Making a trip to find the plant, growing in an area nearby will help you understand the plant's growing patterns and energy without your own influence on it. In most cases harvesting these invasive plants is encouraged. If you prefer to see the plant in its growing cycle from seed to flower, then take extra care to make sure it does not spread. Many invasive plants will impact the area they are introduced to, they will suffocate native plants, or otherwise harm the ecosystem already in place. Some invasive species like the Broom varieties (introduced from all over Europe) are very flammable and can exacerbate forest fires.

   The other end of that is to never harvest rare or endangered plants. Know what you are picking. The spirits that are involved with the plant will not be happy if you take away all of their rare and endemic allies. There are ways to go about this, for example if you know the area is going to be made into condos, than the plant is likely to be destroyed anyway. Or if the area has enough of the plant to harvest a small amount, then it is likely to be fine.

Your own ethical foundation will take form with ongoing cultivation of a relationship with Hekate and your own personal shadow work. Remember that your actions will create results in one way or another. Shadow work is part of the way we can self correct, before we do too much damage.

How are your own ethics part of your practice? How do you honor the plant you harvest from? Do you listen to the environment around you when it says "no" ?

Using Your Voice

Prayer is magic. This seems to be fairly universal, and across traditions and religions worldwide. The sound of your voice ignites the fire of manifestation within your work. The words you say and how you say them, can energetically enhance the work you do. There are many ways to pray, prayer can focus on honoring the plant, or the work, or the action, prayer can focus on the person, or the future, and they can even be coercive, scary or have a threatening tone as well. Remember to honor your ethical code, these are simply examples of how others have worked with plants. Here are a couple of examples from the Greek Magical Papyri . You are encouraged to write your own.

This is an example of a coercive spell to pick a plant.

Greco Roman Egyptian Sorcery: Greek Magical Papyri (30 BCE – 390 CE)

Page 43 in the Betz translation PGM IV. 286-95

*Spell for picking a Plant: Use it before Sunrise. The Spell to Be spoken: "I am picking you, Such and such a plant, with my five fingered hand, I, NN, and I am bringing you home so that you may work for me for a certain purpose. I adure you by the undefiled / name of the God: If you pay no heed to me, the earth which produced you will no longer be watered as far as you are concerned- ever in life again, if I fail in this operation,Mouthabar Nach Barnachocha Braeo Menda Laubraase Phaspha Bendeo; Fulfil for me / the perfect charm." (voces magicae)

An example of a invokation and offering
PGM IV. 2967-3006

*Among Egyptians herbs are always obtained like this: the herbalist first purifies their own body. First they sprinkle themselves with Natron and fumigate the herb with resin from a pine tree after carrying it around the place three times. Then, after burning kyphi and pouring the libation of milk as they pray, they will pull up the desired plant while invoking the name of the daimon (supernatural being) to whom the herb is being dedicated and call upon this daimon for the herb to be more effective for the use in which it is being acquired.

The Invocation which is spoken over the herb at the moment of harvesting is as follows:

"You Were sown by Kronos. You were conceived by Hera. You are maintained by Amon. You were given birth by Isis, you are nourished by Zeus, the God of rain, and you were given growth by Helios and the morning dew.. You are the dew of all the gods. You are the heart of Hermes. You are the seed of the primordial gods. You are the eye of Helios. You are the light of Selene. You are the zeal of Osiris. You are the beauty and glory of Ourano's. You are the soul of Osiris' is Daimon, which revels in every place. You are the spirit of Amon. You have exalted Osiris, so exalt yourself and rise just as Helios rises each day. Your size is equal to the zenith of Helios. Your roots come from the depths, but your powers are in the heart of Hermes. Your fibers are the bones of Mnevis. And your flowers are the eye of Horus. Your seed is pans Seed. I am washing you in resin as I also washed the gods, even as I do this for my own health. You also will be cleaned by prayer and as the power of Aries and Athena do. I am Hermes. I am acquiring you with good fortune and good Daimon both at a perpetuous hour and a Perpetuous day that is effective for all things."

An offering is left in the place of the harvested plant, this offering is 7 seeds of wheat and 7 seeds of barley mixed in honey. Once this offering is given in the ground where the plant once was the herbalist will depart.

The Altar

Your Working Altar to the Goddess Hekate can be in a place indoors or outside, but it needs to be a place accessible to you every day. Some suggestions would be to place her on the highest altar, above all other deities during this work. Another suggestion is to have it be an altar that faces the doorway or a window, so she can see all who enter a space. Ultimately it is up to you and your connection to Her, in where you place it, but remember, this is a working altar, make sure you have access to it.

To create your Altar to work within the realms of this book, these are the items you will need:

An image or statue of Hekate
A tool of the harvest
An altar cloth
A tool of divination: oracle/tarot cards, bone or charm set, etc.
A bell
Mugwort incense or dried herb to burn as incense
A silver-tone bowl that can hold liquid and plant material

The colors associated with Hekate are red, black and white. You should have 3 three-yard cords total, one of each color. These will create a tool for your ordination into this realm of Hekate.

You will also need 3 veils, one of each in red, black and white.

Red is the color of life, from the blood of the womb we are born.
Black is the color of death, the mystery of what is to come.
White is the color of rebirth, the discovery of the soul's true nature

Note on your tool of harvest: it's best to create your own tool, or have a professional create it for you if you are using this for your magical work. The metals mentioned as being of Hekate are bronze and iron. Medea is said to have a sickle made of bronze, and she was one of Hekate's High Priestesses. Hekate is described as wearing "Brazen Sandals" which means they were made of bronze and/or gold. Iron is a stable metal that is common throughout the world and it is metal found in our blood, it is an excellent metal for people who practice different forms of blood magic. Iron was also associated with Hekate and was mentioned in the Greek Magical Papyri in spells using the metal in relation to the Goddess Hekate. These metals will react to whatever they come in contact with and many people's personal preference when working with herbs is to use stainless steel, as it is hypoallergenic and has minimal reaction to plant material. The choice is yours, but I personally have collected several of these tools in different metals, they all work for different things. Be sure to choose the one you feel you can use the most for this practice, you can eventually expand to different metals and tools

Knife: Could be a simple pocket knife or other small knife that is easy to carry. Having a good knife is a great multi tool for your harvest. This is used for harvesting leaves, flowers and sometimes branches.

Hori Hori: A very useful tool for digging up roots, similar to a trowel, the hori hori is typically thinner and can make less impact on the ground around it. These will often have a serrated edge that can help saw through larger roots and stems.

Pruning Shears:Helps cut through particularly hard, dry and tough roots with the least difficulty.

Sickle: This is helpful for the harvesting or the cutting down of grasses without uprooting them. Either to use for food or magic, or to allow more light to reach the plants you are cultivating. It can come in many different sizes. The Harvesting Sickle is helpful for reaching into thorny brush to cut off parts of a plant that may be blocked by thorns. (Also good for harvesting squash.)

Boline: Ritual knives that are used for a specific purpose. Baneful herbs would not be cut with the same blade that you would cut other herbs. A boline is considered a ceremonial blade, and can be made of different metals depending on what its use will be. Bronze and iron seem to be preferred.

Sometimes we find that one of these will have distinct benefits over another, and it is fun to discover the uses of each. Decide on one to start with for the next 3 moons, and if that no longer feels right, you can change to another. I would use caution if you decide to harvest poisonous plants with the same blade you use for your other herbs, it helps to have your blades labeled so they are distinctly different. I have collected many tools of the harvest over the years. I have lost many pocket knives and scissors to the fae in the woods, but I find I can keep the small iron blades attached to my gathering basket when taking longer walks in the wilderness.

As for your tool of divination, you can create your own or purchase something. Think about how it relates to the Goddess Hekate. If it is a tarot deck, why do you connect it to her? If it is something you made, how are the materials used to create something relating to Hekate? You can use anything that will give you guidance in your daily practice. Even a coin is something you can flip to get a yes or no answer, it does not need to be an expensive or overly complicated tool. These questions just ask you to think about why you would place it on her altar and use it in relation to her energy for work with her. This tool will be the divination tool that remains on your altar and is dedicated to work with Hekate. Here are some examples of Tools of Divination:

Tarot
Scrying Mirror
Casting Bone Set
Coin(s)
Pendulum
Runes
Inyx Wheel
Crystal ball

Other items that you may want to procure for growing and harvesting of plants that don't necessarily have to be on the altar:

Gloves: Handy to harvest plants like stinging nettle or blackberry or other plants with thorns or stings. Get yourself a good pair of leather gloves to protect your hands from most thorns.

Gathering Basket: You must have a basket or bag that you can place your gathered or harvested plants in. This can be something simple or elaborate, and may depend on what you are harvesting. Some items do not do well being smashed.

Mortar and Pestle: Used to grind and mix plants for easier use. This is another item that you may use for certain herbs depending on whether they are aromatic, for food, or considered poisonous.

Journal: Document your herbal work throughout the seasons. What a plant looks like can be drawn out for better understanding. How does the taste change throughout the seasons (of non-poisonous plants of course), what about the colors of the plant? What a plant's habits are and where it grows in certain locations are helpful things to track in your work with your plant allies. This can be more valuable over the years as you begin to notice patterns in the weather.

You can add things that are dear to you and represent your path with Hekate, or will help you along this path. Once you have your cloth on the altar (a table, or raised spot in the house where you can have time to yourself undisturbed), place the image of Hekate first and then place everything else on in whatever order you choose. You are preparing for your daily work with this Altar, as well as Full and Dark Moon Magic. You will begin on the next day with your daily practice.

At your Altar this will be your first task:

Poison Hemlock *Conium maculatum*

This plant is a member of the Carrot family and as such can be mistaken for other plants within this realm. Queen Anne's Lace and Parsley are commonly confused for Hemlock. This is a fatal mistake however, and will lead to death even if only a few leaves are consumed. Hemlock is distinct in its spotted branches, smell, and how much juice comes out of the plant itself when cut. It is hollow on the inside and grows taller than Queen Anne's Lace or Parsley. Hemlock was initially brought over to the Americas by the Europeans as an ornamental plant, which quickly became feral. So now you will find it in moist areas near rivers and streams, in open fields, and otherwise feral places. Hemlock was used in Greece to help with suicide and as a means of execution. The most famous to be executed with Hemlock would be Socrates. This plant should not be consumed, it is however used to consecrate ritual instruments. Again **DO NOT INGEST THIS PLANT and USE CAUTION WHEN HANDLING as it can absorb through the skin or cause respiratory issues if the toxic juice sprays on you.**

Hemlock Flower Essence

You need:
A hemlock patch or a fresh piece of hemlock carefully harvested.
Rainwater or spring water
Splash of alcohol for preservation
A jar with lid

Flower essences are a simple way of accessing a plant's energy without poisoning oneself in the process. A flower essence is meant to gather the energetics of the plant without having any of the medicinal compounds present in the elixir. Place your water in the jar and surround the jar with the hemlock; wrap the plant around the jar. The jar will have the water inside it and the lid will be on it. This will be left outside all night, to be uncovered in the morning. Please note, there is absolutely no plant material in the jar, it is wrapped only around the outside of the jar. When you gather the jar in the morning, you will add your alcohol of choice for preservation. 20 percent alcohol is ideal. Hemlock flower essence can be used to consecrate your tool of the harvest, and can be taken to help with personal transformation. Simply add a drop to a glass of water or sprinkle around your ritual space.

Consecrate your blade before you work with it. Remember that this blade's purpose is to cut, it must be treated with respect and only used for your work with plants. Do not touch the sharp edges, and handle it as if it were an ancient relic you somehow have the honor of holding. For this you will need:

Hemlock Flower Essence
A fresh sprig of rosemary
Your tool of the harvest

Make sure you are freshly bathed.

Place 3 drops of the hemlock flower essence on your rosemary sprig and gently wash over each of your hands just before you reach for your blade. As you hold the blade in your hands say the following chant three times:

"For the plants in this holy work
I have this tool of life, death and rebirth.
Consecrate and make new
For this work I will do"

If you do not have Hemlock or do not feel comfortable working with it, you can simply use the rosemary sprig on its own.

Consecrate your body with your rosemary brush and hemlock essence. Begin at your head and move down to the feet. Sometimes this is called "floral acupuncture" Activating parts of your energy system on specific energy points on the body.

Take your rosemary sprig and gently brush the blade with it. When you are done, make sure the blade is fully dry by gently wiping it with a new clean cloth, USE CAUTION and DO NOT cut yourself . You should tell the blade you are grateful for it, and that it will help you on this journey. Place it on your altar.

Daily Practice

It is better to do a little every day, than to attempt to do one large ritual a year. It takes time to build a relationship with this Goddess, and like Saturn, it will take its time. You will write out your own devotional Prayer to the Goddess. This is something that honors The Mighty Queen and your work in the plant world. The Devotional prayer is something you will read every day and it will have its place in an acceptable area on the altar. This is the prayer you will say every day in your work with Hekate.

Your daily Practice will look like this:

As you gaze at your image of the Goddess Hekate

Ring the bell over your head

Deep breath and as you exhale;
One, Two, Three
Deep Breath and as you exhale;
One, Two, Three
Deep breath and as you exhale;
One, Two, Three

Say your devotional~

"Great Goddess Of the void, of creation and destruction
Great eater of the dark, and purveyor of light
Shining down on my path that was once a mystery
You open my eyes to your hidden knowledge
That I may fly beyond this space and time
And into the secret realm of the Pythoness."

"Hekate of the path I invoke thee;
Lovely Lady of the Triple Crossroads
In heaven, on earth, and in the sea,
Lady of the Saffron Robe,
Sepulchral spirit, celebrating the Bacchic Mysteries
Among the souls of the dead,
Daughter of Perses, lover of solitude, delighting in dear,
Nocturnal, Caretaker of Dogs, Invincible Queen.
She of the cry of the beast,
Ungirt and having an irresistible form
Bullherder, Keeper of Keys to all the universe.
Mistress,I pray thee maiden to be present at our hollowed rites.
Always Bestowing thy graciousness upon the Boukolos.
(Orphic Hymn)

When You are done saying your devotional prayers out loud to Hekate you can move to your tool of divination, and ask it for guidance for this day. For your first practice you will want to cleanse your tool of divination before you place it on the altar. Mugwort incense is best for this. Any tool of divination you decide on; tarot deck, oracle deck, pendulum, scrying stone, bone set etc, can be smoked with mugwort to help cleanse and enhance. Be sure to pick one, and only one tool of divination for this altar. Do not switch them out unless absolutely necessary.

Now you have your advice from your tool of divination, You will now do the count down again but like this:
Deep Breath and as you exhale
Three, Two, One
Deep Breath and as you exhale
Three, Two, One
Deep Breath and as you exhale
Three, Two, One

Ring the bell again.

This countdown has many purposes. It will help relax and connect you to the space in which you do your work. Hekate is most associated with the number 3 and counting forward and back can help trigger your mind to get ready for your magical work. The more you do it, the more you will be guided by it, and that is why it is part of your daily practice. When you come to your altar every day you will do your countdown, ring the bell over your head then say your devotional prayer. I encourage you to use the prayers above, and you will be creating your own devotional to the Goddess at the 3rd moon.

OF LIFE

For the Following 3 moons you will wear your 3 yard red cord around your waist every magical working and ritual you do. Wear your red cord for daily practice, and each of the dark and full moons.

"In the Furthest Recesses of the enclosure was a sacred Grove
Shaded by Flourishing trees. In it there were many laurels and
Cornels and tall plane trees. Within the grass was carpeted
with low growing plants with powerful roots. Famous
Asphodel, pretty maidenhair, rushes, galangal, delicate
verbena, sage, Hedge mustard, purple honeysuckle, healing cassidony,
Flourishing field basil, mandrake, hulwort, in addition to fluffy
Dittany, fragrant saffron, nose-smart, there too lion-foot,
greenbrier, chamomile, black poppy, alcua, all-heal,
white hellebore, aconite, and many other noxious plants grew from
The earth. In the middle of a stout oak tree with heaven high trunk spread its branches
Out over much of the grove. On it hung, spread out over a long branch, the golden fleece,
Over which watched a terrible snake." ~Apollonius of Rhodes in the Argonautica

1st Dark Moon

Your belly button was once the physical link to your mother, the remnant of the nourishment that came from the source of your physical flesh. This was your first scar, healing over after a gestational period and through the traumatic event that was your birth. It is as though we hatched from the cosmic egg within the body of the Goddess, a dark warm cave of blood and tissue, to be greeted by a world of pain and light. The transfer of circumstance is shocking and confusing as the physical cord is cut and you learn to access nourishment from the environment around you.

For the first time you do this near the dark of the moon, you will gather fresh plants for her altar. You will take a walk to harvest plants. Take your tool of the harvest off the altar and with you to do this work. Your walk can be long or short; it all depends on where you have been guided. The goal of this walk is to find the most common plants around to create the bouquet. You will not be wild crafting rare, endangered or otherwise illegally obtaining these plants. You will only harvest a small amount at a time. This will help to keep you out of trouble, but is also part of your Ethos. Know that when you harvest from the plant, you will need to give the plant something back. Take an offering to the plant; suggested offerings can be eggs, compost, a song, time tending it, or something that you feel the plant needs. Tell the plant what you are harvesting it for, and carefully take the tool of harvest and cut off a sprig of each plant; you will need to find three sprigs of three separate plants.

Knowing the signs of toxic plants, and which ones grow in your area will be helpful in not poisoning yourself if you choose to bring it into your bouquet. I will leave it up to you, if you feel called to poisonous plants just be mindful of everyone in your household and if they will be drawn to it. (Especially if you have pets, children or nosy adults)

Bring back your plants to the altar of Hekate, Tie the plants together with a natural cord, place the herbs and your harvest tool at the foot of the image of Hekate.

Say the Following:
"Herbs of health and desire,
Of the hedge and the briar;
Of this magic, I require,
Bring forth my inner fire~
Bless me, Goddess I admire."

You will allow the plants to dry on the altar till the Full Moon.

Rosemary Vinegar

Rosemary is known to help with cognitive function and it is also a plant that will help with purification. This wash is gentle for most skin types and those who use it on their hair regularly proclaim it has soothing properties on the skin. Rosemary is known as an antimicrobial and is one of the ingredients in four thieves' vinegar. This is a plant that is found all over the world. Rosemary is used as a hedge plant to protect borders and is available as a culinary herb. You will gather fresh rosemary to create this wash that will help cleanse the body and purify the soul before every rite.

You will need:
1 cup Apple Cider Vinegar
½ cup of fresh rosemary
Your tool of the Harvest

Harvest the rosemary with your tool, and give appropriate offerings.

Combine the two into a jar and shake vigorously. Set aside till the next full moon making sure there is no plant material sticking out of the vinegar. You want the rosemary completely submerged. Then you will strain it on the full moon in approximately two weeks. Please note, if you see any mold or rot, you will need to toss this batch out and make another.

You will combine 1 Tablespoon of this rosemary infused vinegar to one cup of warm water and apply that to your scalp, letting it drop down onto your skin when you bathe before ritual.

1st Full Moon

This magical work should be done by the light of the moon. The Herbs you placed on the altar in the dark moon should be dried enough for this. Prepare the herb by grinding it into small pieces by hand or with your mortar and pestle. With your ground herbs, you can pour clean water over the herbs and as you do so you will say:

> "Blessed by the Goddess,
> Blessed by her Light
> Into the silver bowl
> That burns in the night.
> I offer these plants,
> Found on this path,
> I offer my chants
> In this moon bath.
> Allow my mind to expand
> And my skills to grow
> That my love of her light
> Continues to show. "

Introduce yourself to the energy of these herbs, find out what types of plants they are, and find out what properties they have over the next moon cycle.

Strain the herbs from the water and put the water in a vial with 20 percent alcohol. Place the marc into the compost. The marc is the bulk herb material that is left over after the extraction process.

Prepare yourself for the visualization by finding a comfortable place to sit in front of your altar to the Goddess.

You will be working with this plant spirit Guided by the Goddess Hekate. Use this Visualization to help you find out how that plant will be connected to you and your work this cycle.

You will need a red veil for this portion. I would suggest recording yourself reading this slowly and then playing it back to do the visualization.

Place the Red veil over your head.

The visualization:

Imagine yourself in a place of nature, one of your favorite places to look at plants, this could be a garden, or a wild landscape. With your eyes closed, take steps into this secret place within your mind and allow yourself to breathe in the essence of everything around you. Begin to smell the earth beneath your feet, Reach down in your mind and feel the earth between your fingers, notice its texture, what is this smell? Feel the temperature from it, is it hot or cold? Smell the roots that live beneath the ground and with your mind's eye notice their colors. Is the root red? Is it white? Is it another color? Are they long taproots or Fibrous roots that intertwine with each tendril, are they like hair? Do the roots come up to the ground, do they creep or are they very strong and visual? Are they deep into the ground? Are they parasitic and grow on other plants? Or are they tuberose like a potato or even a rhizome like ginger? Notice all these things, and move your body into the root system and feel them, completely. Feel for the one plant that calls to you, notice it and take note. Gradually move your visualization above ground and to the topsoil that you can see with your eyes, just at your feet. This is the Earth, this is the place within as the first place that comes to mind, allow it to come. Focus on what the environment is. Is it shadowy and dark? swampy and moist? See the plant above ground. It is ok if you do not recognize it yet, simply note its shape and what colors it is, is it large? Does it look healthy? Begin to notice with your senses the life around you, allow the energy of these plants to feel you back, and open yourself up to what plant will come to guide you. Take the time to be in this place, hearing the sounds of this environment, allow yourself to sit in it for a few moments. Feel the moisture or the dryness on your skin, what other sensations are you feeling? You notice as you look to the horizon, a figure moving towards you, this figure as something in their hands and is bringing it to you. You notice as they come closer, she has two dogs at her side, they are big black dogs. They get close and you see them, notice what the Goddess Hekate looks like, as she hands you the item in her hands. Look down and notice what it is. As you look back up, you notice her and the hounds are gone. You give your gratitude and slowly begin to come back into this space. Opening your eyes slowly.

Now you should write down what the item and any descriptive notes about the plant that came to you. You may or may not have a name yet, but you can draw it out, or write what it brought to mind. From now until the New moon you will be looking to obtain this plant that has come to you.

2nd Dark Moon

Magical Ink of Hekate

This blend honors the Goddess Hekate and is helpful to use when creating written charms or written offerings to the Mighty Queen. You will be using this ink at the next full moon and anytime you need help from Hekate.

1 heaping Tablespoon Fully ripe Black nightshade berries (Blackberries can be substituted if need be)
A drop of your blood or strand of hair(optional)
A pinch of dragons blood powder
1 Wormwood sprig
3 drops of Lavender Essential oil

You are encouraged to find fresh Wormwood, grow it. Know someone who grows it or wildcraft it. Harvest it with your tool. If for whatever reason you cannot find it fresh, you can purchase dried Artemisia Absinthium and place your blade on top of it overnight.

In your mortar and pestle specifically for magical use, crush your Dragons Blood into a powder or purchase it this way. Add your black nightshade berries and wormwood sprig. Grind these up and add your alcohol to just cover. Add the 3 drops of Essential Oil of Lavender. This will give you a thin ink that is suitable for magical work with Hekate.

Place on your altar to Hekate and chant over the ink 9 times:

"Hekates scribe, Her Sacred Clerk
Imbibe this ink to do her work
In my hand it will increase in Power
As She Guides me, Hour by Hour."

You can now strain off the mark, (keeping it in is possible, but the herb material can get moldy) and place the ink in a pretty Vial.

During the next two weeks, you will look for a feather, stick or other item as you go about your day that will serve well as a pen to write with this ink.

Create your own blessing prayer for your work. Some more examples:

"Herbs of life and manifestation,
Grant us a time of celebration;
See our hopes and desires come true,
That our path of love may continue~ "

"By the power of the moon and the work of our
hand,
I am blessed by the trees and spirits of the land."

"Herbs we/I pluck with gratitude
For this potion we/I have brewed~
That we/I not allow evil to Collude~
We/I partake of nourishing Food~

Herbs of health and desire,
Of the hedge and the briar;
Of this healing I require,
She brings forth our/my inner fire~
Bless us/me, Goddess we/I admire."

These are Individual honorifics: Songs to the
plants, you can give physical offerings of bone, eggs,
blood, food, manure, and compost. Can be tailored to
what you can offer, and is as varied as an individual and
environment.

Write your own plant prayer.

2nd Dark Moon

You will need:

Your Red Veil
A spice for offering
Mugwort incense to cleanse.

The "Prayer to Selene" from the PGM describes the attributes of the Goddess Hekate. As Hekate is a Goddess of the night and the moon, the following spell is to ask for anything you wish the Goddess to Help you with on your journey from this point forward. Before you begin, make sure you are freshly bathed, and you will burn mugwort incense in your space to cleanse the room. You will need to make an offering of spice at the end. Cinnamon, cardamom, saffron etc. are all suitable choices. You can burn it as incense or place it in an offering bowl or on the image of the Goddess. You can record this and play it back or memorize the whole thing to say it under the veil. As you listen to the words, you can picture the Goddess Hekate and her protective aspects. Then at the end you will make your desires known to her for her guidance.

"Come to me, O beloved Mistress, 3-faced Selene
Kindly hear my sacred chants;
Nights Ornament, Youthful One,
Bringing Light to Mortals

O child of Morn Who rides upon fierce bulls.
O Queen, you who drive your chariot
On equal course with Helios,
Who with the triple forms
Of triple Graces
Dance in Revel with the Stars
You are Justice and the thread of the Fates,
Klotho, Lachesis and Atropos,
O Three-headed One you are
Tisiphone, Megaira and Allecto
Many Formed, who arm your hands
Withdreaded murky lamps,
Who shakes the locks of fearsome serpents at your brow,
Who sounds the roar of bulls from out your mouths
Whose womb is decked out with reptile scales,
And poisonous rows of serpents down your back
Bound across your back with horrific chains.
O Night-bellower, Lover of solitude,
Bull-faced and Bull-headed One
You have the eyes of bulls and the voice of dogs.
Your forms are hidden in the shanks of lions.
Your ankle is wolf-shaped,
and fierce dogs are friendly to you,
And so they call you Hekate, Many-named, Mene,
Cleaving the air like arrow-shooting Artemis,
Night shining, triple sounding, triple headed, triple voiced
Hekate
Artemis, Persephone, Deer-shooter, Night-shiner,
Triple voiced, Three-headed, Thrice-named Selene
And Goddess of the triple way
Who hold untiring flaming fire in triple baskets
You frequent the Crossroad
And rule the triple decades
I am calling! Please be gracious!
and with kindness give heed!

You who protect the world at night
Before whom Daimons Quake
And in fear the Immortals tremble,
O Goddess Who exalts men
You of many names, who watches over the dead
O Bull-eyed One, Horned One,
The nature mother of all things
For you Frequent Olympos
And the broad chasm of the Abyss
Beginning and end are you
and you alone are Mistress of All:
For all things are from you, and in you do all things
Eternal One, come to their end
You bear at your brow an everlasting crown
You wear great Kronos' chains
And you hold in your hands the golden scepter
The letters around your scepter
inscribed by Kronos himself
Who gave it to you to wear
that all things remain steadfast:
Subduer and Subdued!
Conqueror of men!
You rule Chaos, Araracharara ephthisikere,
Hail Goddess and attend your epithets!
I offer you this spice o Child of Zeus
Dart Shooter, Heavenly One, Goddess of Harbors
Who roam the mountains, Goddess of Crossroads
Nocturnal and infernal Goddess of the Dark,
Quiet and frightful, feasting among graves
You with the hair of serpents and serpent girded
You who drink blood
And who feast on the hearts of men, flesh eater
Who devours the dead
Come to my sacrifices,
and now for me, fulfill this matter~

((State What you Want Here))

Make your offering of spice to the Goddess.

PGM IV Betz trans p. 90-92

3rd Dark Moon

Noumenia
The first sliver of the new

Hekate's Deipnon is a meal offered to Hekate and her retinue of Vengeful Ghosts on the new moon. This would be a time you would cleanse the home, and place offerings on the doorstep to appease those midnight travelers. Food made with Garlic, Onions, Eggs, Barley, and/or fish is acceptable. Small round cakes are also a good offering. This is typically done every new moon or Noumenia. To be done on the last day of the dark moon.

Cleansing of the Home

Your Bell
Mugwort leaves
Rosemary sprig (optional)
Charcoal (optional)
A cup of water with a few drops of your magical water in it.
Your food offering

Add some of the herb water that you made earlier in the previous moon to a cup of water and leave it at the door. The bell will also stay at the door.
Beginning at the front door you will ring your bell three times.

Now you will take your dried mugwort leaves and fumigate your living space. If you cannot burn this, you can make a strong infusion of mugwort and dip a rosemary sprig in it to asperge your living space of any evil directed at you and to disperse stagnant energy. You can use a mugwort bundle to burn, or place the dry herb on a charcoal disk in a heat safe container that you can carry around the room. Always practice fire safety when doing this. A seashell will not hold the heat of a charcoal disk and brass can get hot in your hands.

Leave the cup of water and bell at the front doorway entrance; ring it 3 times before you begin. Begin the home cleansing by starting and ending at the front door. Move the smoke in a counterclockwise motion, and move through the house in a counterclockwise motion. Pay extra attention to all the windows, doorways, and any corners or dark areas of the room or house. Take your time, you can play music, sing or be silent, but your energy should be focused on the work in front of you. Sometimes singing and music can help with that focus, but it is up to you and what you are comfortable with. When you are done, you will ring the bell again three times, and you can use the cup of water to put the incense out. You will throw the cup of water out to the nearest crossroad. This will help with the cleansing. When night falls, you can leave a food offering at your doorstep, or the nearest crossroad.

The counterclockwise motion is traditionally a "Banishing" movement.

3rd Full Moon

You will need:
Create a tincture invoking the Goddess into your daily
practice

Calendula flowers
Lavender Flowers
Dandelion petals
Brandy
A pint glass jar

The plant material can be dried or wilted for a few hours,
but the brandy must cover the herbs themselves. Wilting
the flowers will help prevent spoilage in the brandy.
When a plant is wilted it loses moisture, and is less likely
to rot. Harvest the flowers with your tool of the harvest
and pick the petals gently with your clean hands. Make
sure where you harvest from is not sprayed with pesticide
Do not use ingredients if you are allergic to them.
Combine all the ingredients into a jar with a tight lid.
Shake to mix and place on the altar. You will write on a
piece of clean paper with your Hekate Ink What it is you
are working to create more of in your life. This can be a
word that represents something or a picture, it is up to
you, but you must sign it. Take a few moments to sit in
silence and think about what is most important and have a
focus. What is the one thing that you can do to make you
better at what you do? How can the Goddess Guide you
in this process? How are you already taking steps to
create a better place for yourself in the world?

Homer, Odyssey 24. 12 ff (trans. Shewring) (Greek epic C8th B.C.) :

"So did these ghosts travel on together squeaking, while easeful Hermes led them down [to the Land of the Dead] through the ways of dankness. They passed the streams of Okeanos, the White Rock (petra Leukas), the Gates of the Sun (pylai Hêlioi) and the Land of Dreams (demos oneiroi), and soon they came to the field of asphodel, where the souls (psykhai), the phantoms (eidola) of the dead have their habitation."

OF DEATH

For the Following 3 moons you will wear your 3 yard Black cord around your waist for every magical working and ritual you do. The other two cords will remain on the altar. Wear your Black cord for daily practice, and each of the dark and full moons.

There are so many manifestations of Hekate. She is who guided Persephone out of the Underworld and back to her mother, Demeter. This Midwife and Advocate for you in those times of life, death and rebirth; walking with you as witness to the forks in the road that lead you to where you need to be. It takes time, and with her own energy she combines and creates an alchemical mix of decay and nutrients in the winter soil that allow for the prosperity of spring and summer. The energy of this process moves slowly , just like the growth of the roots beneath the Earth. This is Death.

"O Lord Helios and Sacred Fire
The spear of Hekate of the Crossroads
Which she bears as she travels Olympus
And dwells in the triple ways of the holy land
She who is crowned with oak-leaves
And the coils of wild serpents." The Root Cutters, book Sophocles

4th Dark Moon

Create your Poplar oil Extract

After you have done your daily practice on this day and before you countdown from 3-2-1 you will create this oil. It is best to have the ingredients placed on the altar beforehand. You will need:
¼ cup poplar buds (fresh is best, dry will work)
¼ teaspoon At least a 70 percent alcohol
Olive oil to Cover the poplar buds
A Jar
Place the poplar buds in a jar that you will use only for this oil as the resin from the buds will not wash off the glass.
Use the Alcohol intermediary method on the buds (put the ¼ teaspoon over the poplar and shake to mix, leave open overnight and close your daily practice, to finish the next day.
The next day add olive oil to cover and let them macerate from dark moon to full moon on your altar to Hekate. (2 weeks approx)

Poplar is a tree that is associated with death and the underworld, as Homer has noted, Poplar trees grew at the gates of Hades and on the banks of the river Acheron in the underworld. The buds of the poplar are often used in perfumes and ointments due to their warm scent and pain relieving properties, they will exude a sticky, rust colored resin that is aromatic and full of their vital essence. The scent and energy of poplar is said to be calming and encourages peace, a useful plant to help process death and the grieving process. Olive branches are associated with the fire of Hekate's torches according to Porphyry, something that will light a path through the mystery of Death.

4th Full Moon

It is time to strain off your tincture you made at the previous full moon.
You will need:

Cheesecloth or strainer
Equal amount of honey to strained liquid.
Dark bottle to store the syrup.
Measuring cup with pouring spout

Using the strainer or cheesecloth, separate the bulk (AKA the "Marc") plant material and set aside to dry out. Reserve the liquid and mix it with equal amounts of honey. Shaking it in a glass jar will gradually mix the tincture and honey, and you can put your own energy into the mix this way. Be sure to place the lid tightly on the jar and shake vigorously

Say the Following as you shake:

"Above and below,
This honey will flow
Through this light
My magic will grow"

 It helps if the honey is liquid and warming it to body temperature can help with this if it is crystalized. Asphodel honey would be nice but any honey that you can find locally is also wonderful.

This will make a syrup that you can use as offerings and take by the spoonful to help build your connection to the Goddess Hekate. The herbs used in this formula are soothing to digestion but do not take it by mouth if you are allergic to any of the ingredients or have any fear as you take the finished elixir.

Dry the leftover herb mark and you can mix it into your loose incense if desired.

5th Dark Moon

Ghosts will often linger among their tombs, and it is said that you can feel the spirits when walking among the graves of those gone. In ancient Greece, it is said that the particularly active ghosts are those that are considered the restless dead. These are their catagories:

Ataphoi are those who were not given a proper burial

Bi(ai)othanatoi are those dead through violence

Agamoi are those who died unmarried

Aoroi are those who died before their time, often the ghosts of children

Lares is a latin term used to describe those spirits who are the protectors of a family, an ancestor that often will protect its descendants. Known as eudaimones (a guardian spirit) in Greek.

" *[Plotinus (3rd century A.D.)] says, indeed, that the souls of men are demons, and that men become Lares if they are good, Lemures or Larvae if they are bad, and Manes if it is uncertain whether they deserve well or ill.* "

In this space we will be working with Eudaimones or Lares, to bring about blessings for ourselves.

You can create a space in your home to contact spirits of the dead if you are for whatever reason, unable to find an appropriate cemetery. If you know of the person whom you wish to connect with via your blood or affinity you can use their image or an image that represents them instead of being at their gravesite.

Alternatively if you wish to take this outside of your living space or you have access to the perfect cemetery, feel free to find your way there and/or to the gravesite of your choice.

Have your herbal honey as an offering for the chosen dead and a Head of Garlic for Hekate ready. You will need to harvest blackberry vine with thorns all the better if they are harvested at the Cemetery.

Pluck 6 thorns off the blackberry vine and place them around the image or headstone of the person with the point of the thorns alternating, in and out.

"As I protect You, You protect me, we are connected by Heaven, Earth and Sea

In the Earth, the realm Below, come above and see me Now. ,

I call to you, to come to me, within this place, It is

((name of the ancestor here)) I see."

Repeat the Above 6 times.

You will create an altar in honor of this person. Every day you will give them an offering that they enjoy and in turn they will protect you.

5th Dark Moon

You will need
Poplar Oil
A Red and Black Veil
Hekates Ink
A pen
A paper
An offering of round Cake
A small paint brush
Two Black Candles
Equal Parts powdered myrrh, powdered saffron
(calendula can be substituted for saffron if not available)
and powdered rose petals.
Powdered white clay.

Light your candles and place your powdered herbs into a
bowl. Add the clay, and mix well.
Place 3 drops of poplar oil into the powdered herbs and
mix in silence. Then add your water to make an acrylic
paint like consistency. Take your paint brush and dip it
into the clay and herb mixture and then begin to paint it
on, starting on the face, avoiding the eyes. Once you at
least have your face painted you will light your two black
candles. Have your found pen (feather, stick etc.) and ink
ready to write.

Imagine you lived your life in the best possible way, you
have no regrets. What does that feel like? Where was
your favorite place you lived? How did you get there?

Write out your final goodbye onto this piece of paper. You can use a regular pen so as not to interrupt your flow, but sign the paper with your signature in Hekates ink.

Allow the clay to dry

For this visualization you will need your red and black veils.

Place the red veil over your head first and the black over the red.

Record yourself saying the following visualization, and then play it back to better access its message.

You see the earth before you, a tiny planet in a sea of galaxies. You come swirling fast to the place you were born. The ground is open and waiting, seemingly hungry for your flesh. Your life as you know it is done. This is the Great initiation, the path every living soul must take is now before you, Hekate stands with you, ready to lead you through the hungry dark and for a moment she guides you through the high and low points of your life beginning at death to your birth. You see within that the pattern of your life's journey. All you know or think you know is laid out before you. She takes you further through your blood line and you see every life that has brought you into existence. Your ancestors' joy and pain, their very lives become within you.

Lay your physical body down, in what is known as "the corpse pose" . Allow yourself to release the physical for just a moment in this space. Feel the Goddess with you now. Take a few moments to be in this space. What message does she tell you here? What guidance does she offer now?

After you have given some time to release, feel your soul coming back into your body. First move your feet, then wiggle your legs, move each finger, and wiggle your arms. Gently bring yourself up to a comfortable seated position. You may remove the veils if you wish. Now you can bathe your skin in plain water, no soap, but you can use a brush or wash rag if needed. Speak to no one as you take the Round cake and offer it at a crossroad or other liminal space. Consider yourself among the realm of the dead till the sun rises and you will come alive when you hear the bell ring when you do your next daily practice.

6th Dark Moon

The Annoying Bug

Every animal and plant has a reason for coming to you, sometimes that reason is to irritate and annoy you. People can be like that too; they can be like that annoying tick, flea or mosquito that you try to avoid so as not to become food for a parasitic or otherwise opportunistic creature that can carry disease.
This is a bit of sympathetic magic that you can use at any dark moon, but now as your powers begin to become stronger in this work. You may notice a jealous or advantageous person(s) trying to siphon or subdue your work. Please note: this ritual will remove these obstacles from your life.

You will need:
An annoying bug like a tick, flea, mosquito, etc
Poppy seeds
A ball of mud
A moving river
A piece of paper
A pen
A name of a specific person who is creating trouble for you.

This bug represents one annoying person who is vexing your situation; it is the energy they bring to you. This is a person who acts as a parasite or a controlling jealous type. The poppy seeds are known to subdue and keep shit talkers silent, when they seek to manipulate and control you. The mud binds them and keeps them in an unmoving state. The river controls where they go now and it should be moving away from you and your home. The poppy seeds will bring birds that will eat them, and also annoy the annoying bug.

Write the person's name on the paper three times and say the following

"Let the water carry you
Away from me,
let the birds pick at you,
Seed by seed. "

Take the ball of mud and stuff the strip of paper into it, followed by the physical bug. Press the paper and bug in the middle of the ball of mud surrounding it with the mud, then press in the poppy seeds on the outside. Throw the ball of mud into the moving river, turn away and do not look back.

6th Full Moon

Creating an Ointment for prophetic dreaming:

Add 3 star anise crushed in mortar and pestle
Add Mugwort to fill the 4 ounce jar
Add Your Poplar oil to cover herbs

~Optional : (for the poplar buds: Alcohol intermediary method : place all the poplar in the jar, and add a few drops of Ethanol to coat all the poplar in the jar, cover and shake the alcohol so that it coats all the herbs. Leave the herb jar open overnight (but covered with a cloth to keep out insects), this will allow the alcohol to do its extraction work and once that is done it will eventually evaporate, leaving the medicinal components behind. Then add your oil the next day.

This gives your preparation a little more potency as the alcohol will extract different constituents than the fat will and it will add another layer of natural preservation.~

Let infuse for at least one moon cycle.

On the Full Moon this can be buried in a place where it will remain undisturbed and where the sun has the potential of heating it under the soil. Make sure the lid is tight and moisture will not get inside, also do not do this if the soil is freezing.

Create a charm to bless your work or use one of the following:

"Bless this ointment and the plants and animals whose essence lies within~
bless these hands who create it, and bless whose skin it touches.
May they see what will help them to become their highest self,
And may they strive to create a better world with their knowledge."

"These Herbs :Poplar, Mugwort and Star Anise
Are blessed with the power to transform
Confusion into Clarity,
Ignorance into Knowledge
Doubt into Confidence
I hold in my hand these blest herbs,
I bless the hands that prepared them
and the work I prepare here;
Give me the visions I seek (say what you wish to know more about here)

Of Rebirth

The Guiding light of the Goddess shines brightly now for you to see the path ahead. You have been through Life and Death, now is the time to reignite your inner passion. What has been destroyed will now give way to the new and these lessons to come will guide you on your path. Even if you are afraid, you must move forward. Hekate will show you the path through her torchlight. Now is the time to walk in the self you create, not swayed by being disliked, and open to your true self. This is Rebirth.

For the Following 3 moons you will wear your 3 yard white cord around your waist every magical working and ritual you do. The two other cords will remain on the altar. Wear your white cord for daily practice, and each of the dark and full moons.

"There are Laurel Boughs and aromatic plants; Some brass plates engraved with unknown letters, Tufts of lambswool dyed purple; nails from a gibbet still bearing traces of human flesh. Skulls half eaten by wild beasts, fragments of fingers, noses and ears torn from corpses; entrails of Victims stolen from temples; flasks in which stored the blood of men who had died a violent death, A waxen figure of the goddess Hekate painted white, black and red; holding a whip, a lamp and a sword intertwined by a serpent. Several vases, Some full of water from sacred fountains, others of milk and mountain honey." Anacharsis in his description of the working space of a witch of Hekate.

7ᵗʰ Dark Moon

You will need 3 paper face masks
Myrtle
Mugwort
Sage
Find more local fresh herbs and flowers for adornment of
your masks
Mud or paint to paint the masks if desired.
1 large pole or branch of an appropriate tree to place the
masks on.
Durable red yarn or jute
A hole puncher

When you are able to hold something in your hand that
will trigger a good thought or memory, it can be very
valuable to your magical work. This item you are about
to create is to be symbolic of the Goddess Hekate at the
crossroad. The Crossroad is A path consisting of three
different ways to travel. Hekate is known to haunt areas
of liminality or spaces on the edge between worlds. In
ancient times you might have found a triple faced mask at
the crossroad, where you would leave offerings and ask
for advice on which road would be best to travel.

Take a walk to harvest fresh herbs and plants for your
mask. The above herbs are some suggestions, but feel
free to use what is available in your environment and
season. Let the Goddess Guide you to the plant she
wants.

To begin; you can paint your masks if needed and then you will want to punch holes in the sides, top and bottom of the mask. To re-enforce the hole you can add tape to both sides and make the hole again with a sharp knife. You will tie each mask together side by side first and then tie the top hole to the top of the pole. Use the bottom holes to stabilize the mask so the eyes are staring forward. Since it is paper it is delicate and should be treated as such. Once it is steady you can tie bundles of your plants to dry at the gaps in the sides of the mask. You can place the herbs inside the masks, if you want to. Place this pole in a corner with one face to the doorway and do your house cleansing, sweeping the things you don't want in the house, out the door. Keep this Hekate Pole in the corner till the full moon in two weeks.

Crescent Moon Journey

To be done on the Crescent Moon:

This is A recipe for Incense from Praeperaratio Evangelica as told by Hekate herself to call on the Goddess in your Dreams.

"My image purify, as I shall Show
Of wild rue form the frame and deck it o'er
With lizards such as run about the house
These mix with resin myrrh and frankincense,
Pound all together in the open air
Under the crescent moon, And add this vow.

'Then she set forth the vow, and showed how many lizards must be taken:

Take lizards many as my many forms,
And do all this with care. My spacious house
With branches of self-planted laurel form.
Then to my image offer many a prayer,
And in thy sleep thou shalt behold me nigh."

A suitable substitute for lizard tails is crushed barley mixed with a small amount of honey and 3 leaves of pennyroyal.

Praeperaratio Evangelica, Eusebius

You will need:

You will need:
Mortar and pestle
½ teaspoon Myrrh resin
Teaspoon Frankincense
Sprig of Rue herb
A branch of Laurel
Laurel Leaf
3 Barley Grains
3 leaves of pennyroyal
A small amount of honey (Half a pinky nail amount)

A suitable substitute for lizard is crushed barley mixed with a small amount of honey and 3 leaves of pennyroyal.

The reason for this substitute is that not all of us have access to lizards around our house, and it may go against your ethics to use animal parts. The suggested substitution is crushed Barley mixed with a small amount of honey and 3 leaves of pennyroyal. This is the base for the drink Kykeon, which Demeter threw onto Askalabos for his disrespect which made him turn into a lizard.

In your Hekates Ink Write on the bay leaf "Hekate" three times

Grind your resins by hand using your mortar and pestle. Then begin to add the laurel (bay)Leaf with Hekate written on it, barley, pennyroyal and rue, with the honey being added at the end. This will create your loose leaf incense. You will burn it before you sleep to connect with the Goddess Hekate in your dreams. If you cannot burn incense for whatever reason, then I would suggest keeping it in a small jar where you can pour olive oil onto the mix to cover it completely. Then you can apply the oil before bed to take part in this practice.

How to burn loose leaf incense:

You will need a charcoal disk, these come in different shapes and sizes, but I generally recommend the Japanese Bamboo Charcoal disks as they do not have chemicals in them to help ignite the charcoal, but any incense charcoal will work. You will need a fire safe container like an iron cauldron, or metal sensor that you can put the charcoal disk on safely. First you will light the coal using a lighter and holding the charcoal with metal tongs. You will want the coal to have a ring of gray around it, then you are ready to add a pinch of the loose incense mix.

When you have fully bathed and cleansed yourself and you are ready. Go to your Altar to the Goddess and prepare yourself for this rite.

As you burn your incense your will say this chant:

"Guide me here in this place of Dreams
Lead me through the Gates of Horn
That I may know the truth of things
And I will be reborn."

Now as you sleep you will receive a visit from the
Goddess Hekate or one of her messengers.

7th Full Moon

Now is the time to strain your Oil from the last full moon. This will be anointed to your body before you do the following ritual of Hekate's Pole.

As you strain the herbal marc from the oil, chant the following three times:

> "Dream a dream of a life made new,
> Grant me a clear vision of what to do;
> Open my eyes to see without and within,
> So that I may know my otherworld Kin"

Apply the Ritual Ointment to the back of your neck, chest and hands before moving to the next ritual.

Now you will be taking the Pole you created on the last dark moon and finding a place where it will offer protection for the neighborhood or area with which you live. This will be a three way crossroad of some sort that you feel will be appropriate. This is an area where you know you can regularly tend to if needed. You will need a head of Garlic, 3 eggs, and 3 one dollar coins (or equivalent currency)
Once you have found the spot, you can place the pole and say the following as you leave your offerings;

"Goddess of the night,
Guide us by your light
Of the path and of this road
Of Snake, Horse and Toad
I call to you and ask you for guidance
That no one here be met with violence."

Say your own daily practice prayer that you have written
to the Goddess and walk away, do not look back.

8th Dark Moon

Hekates Rebirth Oil
Ingredients:
Mugwort leaves for incense
Poplar, star anise and mugwort infused oil strained on the full moon.
Lemon essential oil 1 ml
Labdanum essential oil .5 ml
Frankincense essential oil .5 ml
Cypress essential oil 1 ml
10ml bottle

First cleanse your space and the bottle with mugwort smoke. Then you will combine the essential oils into the 10ml bottle and fill to the top with the poplar infused oil.

To blend, place the cap on your bottle and shake as you say:

"With hounds at her side, and her blade in hand,
I gather the knowledge grown on the land
I see the oceans tumultuous waves,
In them the spirits who dove to their graves
I gather their knowledge that lives in my blood
To bring forth the power of the leaf and the bud
Message in the clouds, In a changing sky
I see the vision with my witch's eye.
Like the seeds on the wind through the soft breeze
This is my Rebirth, like new leaves on the trees."

You will apply this oil to the base of your neck during daily practice from this point forward.

Please keep in mind that essential oils are strong extractions of the fragrant chemical constituents of a plant and should always be diluted, this is why you mix it with a carrier oil in this case this is the infused magical oil.

Rue Water
3 sprigs of Rue
½ cup river water from a flowing river
½ cup vodka

A pint sized jar

Place your rue in the jar and then pour the water and vodka over it to cover. Shake three times and say this chant:

"Herb of Grace
Be in this place
Infuse this work
& Bless this space."

Let infuse overnight on the altar then strain for use in house protection work, to consecrate iron tools, and/or to help increase psychic visions. River water is used to help the work to "Flow" it will break up stagnant energy and allow for open paths when combined with the rue.

8th Full Moon

You will need your tool of the harvest.
Mugwort incense

Burning your incense you will begin by standing at your altar to the Goddess. You will be cutting away any negative energetic attachments that may be holding you back in this work. You will start by holding your tool of harvest carefully (You will not be cutting yourself with it) Starting at the top of your head and down to your feet. Imagine as you start at your head you are cutting away those people or situations that live in your head rent free. You are releasing them. You are not allowing their negativity to attach to you from this point forward. Now you will move down to your shoulders and release the burdens placed on you, you will no longer hold onto the weight of the world here.

Moving down to your chest and arms, you will release a loved one that has attached to your heart and yet still seek to harm you or keep you from being successful due to their own issues.

Continue to move down your body, and at each body part, release the trauma associated with it. If you have injuries, pay special attention to those areas and allow your tool to energetically cut away expectations and any other attachments that do not serve you emotionally. When you get down to your feet, you will energetically push all of this suffering and attachment into the earth, away from you. Bring yourself down to the ground and fully feel your emotions, sit with them and be witness to them. This exercise is often repeated because the attachments can come back or new ones are created and they need to be released. Notice in the following days if these attachments come back, and repeat this exercise as needed.

For this full moon rite you will need:
Rue water
Hekates Rebirth oil
2 White candles

Make sure you have bathed in Rosemary Vinegar before you begin.
Cleanse your space with the rue water by dipping rosemary sprig into the water and asperge the area with the water and place it in your working area.
Anoint your white candles with Hekate's Rebirth oil. (Anointing is when you start at the top of the candle and bring the oil down to the bottom.)

First place the Red Veil over your head, then place the Black Veil over your Head, and finally for this visualization you will place the white veil over the top of those two. You can record yourself saying the following slowly and then play it back to do this visualization;

Take in a deep breath, and as you take in a breath let it fill your lungs all the way to the bottom. Breathe in the scent of the Rue water, the Rebirth Oil and the air around you. And as you release our breath, allow your muscles to relax, your jaw to soften, your shoulders to drop. Do this breathing exercise two more times to allow yourself to be fully in this space of rebirth.

Take the following moments to think about what it means to release everything and start new. Without the weight of the limitations placed on you by others, without the burdens they might throw onto your back. Imagine you are in a dark cave, and in this cave is complete darkness. There are only echoes of the sound of your feet as you slowly and carefully walk through the cavern. Soon you see a light, it gradually becomes brighter and you begin to notice that it is a woman carrying two flaming torches. She gets closer and closer to you as you stand in awe of the energy that emanates from her. She is cloaked in a saffron robe, covering her face, but you know she is the Goddess Hekate. She gestures for you to come forward and step onto this path. She gives you her hand and you begin traveling to the surface. You feel weightless and your worries are left behind as you fully trust this energy that guides you on the path. She takes you to a field of light, where you see your ancestors in their own lives. Do not be afraid of them, look to them and see how you have created your own unique existence and now move toward the freedom of the soul that comes with your connection to Hekate…

What does it feel like to begin fresh? Are the fresh wounds of your former attachments that have been cut away hurtful and sore? Or do you feel as though you are instantly transformed? In many cases the transformation has a painful separation period, one that heals and grows into its own power in time. Where do you feel you are in this process?

Transformation can be painful, but ultimately worth it in the end.

9th Dark Moon

For this dark moon rite you will need:
Fresh red rose with thorns
wormwood
The herbal waters that you made on the first dark moon.
A piece of paper and Hekates Ink you made on the dark moon
The Feather/stick/or penlike item You found from Dark moon to full moon.
Two Black candles

First you will dip the roses into the herbal water and sprinkle yourself from head to toe in it. Crush the wormwood between your palms releasing the fragrance of them and place them in the bowl on your altar. Take three thorns off the rose stem and place one on each candle facing out and one in the middle of the candles pointing away from you.

Draw the symbol of Oroboros on the paper with Hekate's ink, the snake eating its tail, and inside you will write :

 Protect my body, Protect my soul, I am ((say your name)) Child of Hekate! 3X

"Hekate I ask you, transform any curses, evil and hatred that have been directed at me into energy that I can use for my own benefit, and anything that cannot be transformed, be sent into the Earth to be destroyed."

Light your Black candles and say the following out loud three times:

Protect my body, Protect my soul, I am ((say your name)) Child of Hekate! 3X

Pass your ouroboros between the two candles as you say the above.

Now you can take this paper charm and carry it with you for additional protection from the Goddess Hekate.

PGM VII. 579-90

9th Full Moon

Braiding of the Cord.
You will need :
Your red, black and white cords
Hekates Oil
A red, black and white candle.

Find a comfortable place to work at your altar.
Sometimes this is on the ground in front of it, or standing
at it, it is up to you.
Light your candles and hold the cord in your
hands and pass them between each, winding like a snake
through each candle from left to right.
When you are done you should have all three
cords in front of you. Begin to anoint each cord;

With the Red Cord, anoint it and say;
"Hekate as Divine Creatrix manifested my soul
and I am brought to Life"

With the black cord, anoint it and say
"I am protected by the Goddess Hekate and I
release those things that seek to harm me"

With the White Cord, Anoint it and say:
"I am reborn and I follow the light of the torches
of Hekate"

Once you have each cord anointed you will begin to braid them together. Begin by knotting the top.
As you are braiding you will chant or sing:

> Hekate Hekate Hekate
> Queen of the Crossroads Hekate,
> Hekate Hekate Hekate
> Mistress of Magic Hekate
> Hekate Hekate Hekate
> Bring us together Hekate
> Hekate Hekate Hekate…
> Light my path Hekate
>
> Hekate, Hekate, Hekate….

This is your cord, where it has collected the energy of your work within this book and your work with Hekate. You can decorate the ends as you please, placing tassels, charms or roots at the ends when you feel you have made progress. Continue your daily practice and repeat the exercises as you feel need to be repeated. Remember that Life, Death and Rebirth is not a linear concept, it is a continued movement, carrying the energy from one to another for all time. You may experience each of these at any moment, in the many aspects of your life. For the sake of this journey, continue with your own works to build a relationship with the Goddess Hekate and learn more wisdom of remedies and poisons.

You can continue with the daily practice and further your education into the plant world. The following portions of the book can help you expand your work with Hekate and plants.

Journey to the Nocturnal Realms

I enter the nocturnal realms
The liminal space between
Within the garden of shadows
I see the mighty Queen
In this place she plucks a rose,
The most beautiful I've ever seen,
She reminds me of the thorns that grow
At the stem of this little being.
"Remember that you too grow,
In a world of duality,
That whosoever plucks the pretty rose,
Can be met with Brutality"

Hekate is often mentioned as a goddess that is associated with dream work, she is a Goddess of prophecy and divination, as well as one who teaches us the ways of herbs and how to use them magically.

Oneiromancy is the first type of divination witches experience; it is also the most common. It requires no tools other than your mind. Since you spend more than 30% of your life sleeping (on average) and it is likely you sleep for 6-8 hours a day, you have ample opportunity to work on the realm of dreams. I encourage you to read through the descriptions as follows and look into the herbs and stones mentioned here. They can be guides for you if you need them in your dream work. Some are easier to acquire than others, depending of course on what environment you live in.

Many people notice that when they begin to really look into enhancing their own psychic powers, they begin to open themselves up on a regular basis. However, it should be noted that when you are in the liminal space of wakefulness and dreaming, you are vulnerable and need to have firm boundaries about what you allow in. How you dream, what you dream, who you dream of, can all determine your own spiritual health. It can tell you if you have gone through trauma, you are cursed or blessed, it can tell you if you have spirits watching over you, it can tell you if you are innocent or guilty, or otherwise need to change your ways or keep walking the path ahead of you. Be sure your ethics are aligned with your desires and also aligned with the actions you do to get what you want.

Oneiromancy:

According to Homer the Oneiroi (Roman; Somnia) are bat-winged Daimones that come from the caves of eternal darkness. The Oneiroi passed through one of two gates~ the gate of Horn that will bestow the prophecies from the Gods and gate of Ivory that will produce false dreams and visions. The names of the Oneiroi are Morpheous(morphing), Phantasus (phantasm), Icelus(resembling) and Phobeter (to be feared) and they are the sons of Nyx and Hypnos. Their story reminds us that there are ways to invite those Oneiroi that have passed through the gates of Horn. The term for this type of divination is Oneiromancy.

Types of Dreams:

What is a NightMare? We have all at one point taken a ride on this Mare, She often comes at night, and she sheds light on some of our deepest fears in our most vulnerable space. The Old Nightmare can consist of more intense bouts of Sleep Paralysis or the more common bad dream. Night Mares often come to us in times of stress or after trauma of some sort. Children will often have a nightmare when they see something scary in a movie. Sometimes these nightmares can feel foreboding as they can feel like they are sending you a message of the future.

Sleep Paralysis or Being Hag ridden is a terrifying experience. You are lying in bed, unable to move, often there is a buzzing type of music vibrating in the area, you may feel like you are being held down, strangled and/or you have a "dark visitor" that manifests itself from the shadows of your sleeping area. Common hypnagogic visions are of small green ghouls, incubus or succubus types or skeletal witch women. But Atonia, or muscle paralysis happens every night when you fall asleep, and it is meant to keep you from moving your physical body while you experience dreams. This natural period of immobility happens for most people, unless you experience Sleep Paralysis's twin: Sleep Walking. Which is when you do not experience atonia, and you are moving your physical body in relation to your dreaming mind. Both are considered relatively common sleeping disorders. Sleep paralysis will likely affect 40% of people at least once in their lifetime, and often it is associated with spirit possession, alien abduction or a restless spirit of some type in folklore. Do not let the scientific description scare you or let you think this is normal or insignificant though, science still does not know why this happens. There is a message in this type of experience, oftentimes it is a sign that you need to do some work on your boundaries, take better care of your stress levels, and assess the people around you who may not have your best intentions at heart. There is also opportunity to call on your protective guides: The Goddess Hekate and Angelos are often terrifying but they may offer themselves as a guide in your dreaming, so that you are a little more protected from errant energy and spirits. Sleep paralysis often comes with the practice of enhancing your psychic powers, and you can cancel these powers completely or begin to move through the fear, and Use it. It should be known that oftentimes when we begin to work in the spiritual world, we are open and inviting to ALL spirits and dreams. This is part of that learning experience. We learn what our boundaries are, and even though Sleep Paralysis is described as the most terrifying experience ever, there are ways to call on your own "Helpers" No matter what your religious background. Find a guide that will help you, otherwise if you want to dampen your psychic ability so as not to experience this, place camphor under your bed in a bowl of water, and you can also burn the blocks of camphor on a charcoal disk in your bedroom.

Lucid Dreaming is dream control. In your dream, you are aware of the fact that you are dreaming, and so you can create your own world within the dream. This takes practice, and a bit of grounding. A problem for many lucid dreamers is that when you find out you are dreaming you will wake up. Remaining calm will help to keep the dream world available to you for your own manipulation. Have an item that you can manifest once you know you are dreaming, this can be a symbol, some kind of talisman or something common like an orange. This is something that you cannot mistake for anything else, it is your good luck charm and it is the first step in manifesting your own dream world. Does the orange help you fly? Does it offer protection from evil spirits or other attackers? Is it strong in scent? Does its color change? Learn to know what you want from your item.

You should be dreaming regularly, although if you have problems remembering your dreams, or they are terrifying experiences you can look into the following herbs and stones that can help in your work with dreams.

Stones:

Moonstone : A feldspar that is used magically to increase powers of divination, aid in dream recall and soothe emotional upset. Helpful to keep near your sleeping area to protect you during your lucid dreaming.

Labradorite : Feldspar sometimes called "Black Moonstone" or "Rainbow moonstone" This is a stone that will help increase intuitive ability. It is said to be the captured lights from the Aurora Borealis. Traditionally used to bring about good mental health, increase magical power and is known to have a calming influence.

Selenite: A soft stone that will slowly dissolve if placed in water due to its high salt content. Used for clearing out negative energy and cleansing, similar aspects to salt and often placed in doorways and windows to cleanse people and entities coming in and out. It can be placed under or over the bed to help protect from negative energy, entities and nightmares.

Celestine: Is a stone made up of strontium sulphate and is traditionally used to help focus the mind. This stone will help to keep you within your body while also able to connect with the spirit world. This is an Excellent stone for people who may have issues with controlling Sleep Paralysis.

Herkimer Diamond: The clarity of this stone and the power it has in dreamwork is well known. It is used to help with lucid dreaming, and can clarify a specific situation you may have in your life through your dreams. This can be made into an essence easily, but can be worn when sleeping or kept near the dreamer by their bedside for dreamwork.

Amethyst is a calming stone that is helpful for people who have insomnia. It is used in dreamwork to open up your subconscious and allow for vivid dreams and dream control. It is called the "Sobriety Stone" In Greek myth, Amethyst was used to stop Drunkenness. The stone got its color from the red wine stained tears of Dionysis when his love interest named Amethyst was turned into a quartz crystal.

Hagstone: Traditionally these stones are found on the beach or shoreline, and sometimes at rivers and streams. These are a stone that has a naturally formed hole in it. The hole was created by the strength of the water and the stone is considered protective. You can also look through the hole and witness the faerie realm. Some say it will reveal to you who seeks to harm you. These are stones that should not be purchased, but naturally found. They are traditionally used to overcome curses and prevent nightmares and Hag riding.

Apophyllite : Used by psychics to increase ability, these stones are often placed alongside tools of divination and worn on the body when seeking to access your powers of intuition. This is an excellent stone for professionals who work in divination and is a helpful tool to have for dreamwork and connecting with messengers (angelos).

Lodestone: Can help with attachments and releasing grief, this stone will attract what you want. Was known as a "Breathing Stone" due to its magnetic actions, the ancients believed it could breathe. Think of how the body breathes in what it needs and releases what it does not. In the PGM there is a spell to carve a triple faced Hekate on a lodestone and use it for protection.

The Dream World

Here are some Herbs used to help with the various aspects of dream work. Some are easier to find than others, and they may not all be mentioned in historical sources on Hekate, but are used by her Devotees as they explore their own environment and plants available to them. These are your list of options with herbs to work with to encourage dreaming. Everyone is different so you are encouraged to look into each of these herbs and see if one is right for you. You may not need any at all. There are some recipes listed with some of the herbs, but you can create your own after understanding contraindications and benefits.

Mugwort: Moon/Venus Various types of mugwort : *Artemisia Vulgaris(Common Mugwort), Artemisia Douglasiana(California Native), Artemisia Argyi (Chinese Mugwort)* Mugwort is the most common herb used to induce dreaming worldwide. It is something easily accessible and is dual duty; it has been shown to promote dreaming and is used to help protect.- Of the several types of mugwort mentioned here they all have similar uses. In acupuncture Mugwort is used to clear blocked energy in the meridians and allow for proper flow, this is done by using "Moxa" which is the prepared mugwort made into an incense and burned on the energy spots in the body believed to be blocked. Mugwort tends to grow near rivers and marshes, usually enjoying habitats that are moist and near flowing water. While often it is stated that mugwort has an affinity for Venus, I can see it influenced by the energy of the moon as well. Mugwort looks into the mystery beyond the realm of consciousness and has a watery emotional aspect to it. Mugwort is known to help promote menstrual flow, so it is not recommended internally for the pregnant or for someone who already has a heavy menstrual flow. Mugwort was also used in transference magic, you would make a crown or belt of mugwort and then wear it for a season, allowing it to protect you from errant spirits and your own bad judgment, at the end of summer you would allow it to absorb any of your bad luck. Then you would throw it into the pyre to effectively transfer all your negative energy into the mugwort to be destroyed. In dream work, mugwort is hung over the bed in a bundle, the fragrance of the plant not only is relaxing, but it will certainly promote lucid dreaming. The fresher the bundle the better, but once it dries out and loses much of its scent, you can then burn it as an incense in your bedroom or other sleeping area to release the essence and promote dreaming once again. Natural Abortifacient, avoid if pregnant.

Xhosa Root, *Silene Undulata, Silene Capensis*, Ubulawu, White Paths or also called African Dream Root is Native to South Africa. African Dream root is traditionally harvested in the second year, and made into a decoction to induce vivid dreams and increase sensitivity to Spirits of the deceased. Traditionally used in the Xhosa Peoples Death Ceremonies some of which being the Xhosa Mourning Ritual where a Cow, Goat or Ox is slaughtered. The Animal is first rubbed with the mixture of ritually prepared Silene Capensis froth. The attendees of this ritual also drink the mixture of Silene Capensis before the ceremony takes place. The animal is then eaten and the new ancestor is honored. Before the funeral an elder will talk to the spirit of the deceased (who still is in the dead body) and guide them to the realm of the afterlife. Mourners are likely to experience visions of this ancestor and receive messages with the help of the dream root, all of which are considered significant and can tell the elder a lot about the journey of the newly deceased.

In traditional uses of this root it is mentioned that the dream root is not only consumed but used as a topical application at the same time. This is used to help connect to the ancestors through dreaming. The dream root not only has been used in rituals of death, mourning and to access the subconscious through dreams but in healing of mental disturbances, releasing toxic habits, toxic attitudes and to help improve brain function.

Walnut *Juglans spp*

Walnut is not directly associated with Hekate throughout history, but walnut is a tree of such great magical potential that it should be mentioned here. The Black walnut is a slightly more bitter tree native to the United States and the common English walnut is native to Persia. Both are said to stimulate the brain and can help to encourage dreaming.

There are several ways to use walnuts for ritual and I have found The Mighty Queen Hekate does like an offering of the traditional Italian Green walnut elixir called Nocino.

Hekates Nocino Recipe

Green Walnuts picked around the summer solstice In multiples of 7.
For every 7 green walnuts add:
 3 crushed star anise
A tablespoon of roasted carob (or coffee)
3 saffron strands
3 cloves
¼ teaspoon vanilla extract
A pinch of nutmeg powder
1 cinnamon stick
` 1 sliced blood orange

You will need Vodka or other preferred spirit.

Add all the ingredients to an appropriate sized jar, fill to the top to cover with Vodka or other preferred spirit. (Vodka has a neutral flavor that won't add to the liquor but you can choose whatever 40-60 percent alcohol you prefer or feel Hekate would enjoy)

Let the plant material infuse into the alcohol for 3 months, then strain. Add half the amount of honey or white sugar to the liquid that is 1 part sugar and/or honey to two parts of the alcohol extract.

Let sit for another 3 months to mellow out and age.

This can be taken as an aperitif to help digest meals and as a drink to share with the Goddess and encourage your power of divination through dreams.

For those who wish to stay away from alcohol as offerings here is a simple recipe for syrup. This would also work well as an offering or mixing into tinctures, oxymels or infused honey.

Green Walnut syrup

Quarter green English walnuts and cover with white sugar.

Let sit for 3 days and then pick out the walnut pieces.

Use the syrup like honey to add to teas, as offerings or in magical elixirs.

Blue Lotus *Nymphaea caerulea* Commonly known as Blue Lotus, it is not actually a lotus but a water lily. When the tomb of Tutankhamun was opened the pharaoh's body was found covered in a mass of 3000 year old blue water lilies. This lily was often placed in wine to enhance the effects. Used as a sleep aid and anxiety reliever Blue Lotus is considered a sacred plant that was often depicted in Egyptian artwork for use in ritual and for divine inebriation. Used before bed this flower can encourage lucid dreaming and a deeper connection to the other side.

Blue Lotus Smoking Blend:

½ ounce Mullein leaves
½ ounce Blue Lotus Flowers
¼ ounce rose petals

Lightly garble each herb individually. (Garbling simply means to put in your blender to create a balanced blend with uniform pieces that will make it easier to smoke)

Blue lotus can be made into a tea, tincture and/or smoked to encourage lucid dreaming and may have psychoactive effects.

Bobinsana *Calliandra angustifolia* is a plant found in the Amazon rainforest and is traditionally made into a tincture (alcohol extraction usually with Aguardente) but is also made as a decoction for strength and energy. Not at all mentioned as an herb related to Hekate in historic text, but a valuable one that grows outside of the mediterranean. The decoction can be drunk to help heal the heart and It is often used with ayahuasca in healing ceremonies. Used to promote lucid dreams, it can bestow empathy for others, and Bobinsana can provide a boundary against energy that seeks to take advantage of that empathic being. The energy of this tree is strong and flexible, it is an enchanting plant that will help to open your heart but allow you to remain deeply rooted in self. Bobinsana grows near rivers and fresh water and is called "Sirenita Bobinsana" , this plant that is said to have the spirit of a mermaid. She is a singer and an artist, and encourages us to not close our hearts and become hard by our experiences, but to find a place for your pain to live that is not inside your body, be it through art, writing or music. Interestingly enough Bobinsana is used medicinally for joint, bone, arthritis pain, uterine problems and to cleanse the blood. Used as a contraceptive as well so avoid it if you want to be pregnant.

Bobinsana tincture folk method:
½ cup ground bobinsana bark
1 vanilla bean chopped
2 cups Organic Cane Alcohol (ETOH), Aguardente or Moonshine. 190 Proof
½ cup Honey
½ cup of water
Green Opal or other healing stone
Small piece of wax paper
A Quart jar

Place the vanilla bean in a blender with the alcohol and fully blend the bean. Add the bobinsana to the jar and pour the alcohol over it, stir the mixture and let sit in a cool,dark place. This alcohol is extremely flammable, do not put it near a fire or a very warm area, like near a stove or candle. You can use the piece of wax paper to separate the underside of the lid from the liquid as the high proof alcohol will react to the metal in the lid of the jar. Place your gemstone on top of the lid of the jar to imbibe with its healing essence. You will allow this to infuse for one full moon cycle, shaking the jar every day to help release the medicine and put your energy into the tincture. At the end of the moon cycle you will strain off the bulk material or "marc" and keep the liquid. The Marc can be dehydrated to make tea, or placed in a cauldron to burn and make into witches salt. Once you have your liquid, you can add a half cup of honey and a half cup of water, mix well and take 30-60 drops in water when you are ready to process your traumas. I would use it for up to 2 weeks at a time, and eat plain foods while you do.

Poplar/Cottonwood is in the same family of trees as the Willow and both contain the constituent "Salicylic acid" which is where we get our modern aspirin from. It was traditionally used in flying ointments likely due to its pain killing properties. Many ingredients in these preparations were also known to be pain relieving when applied topically. The energy of poplar is said to invoke peace and is often used in reconciliation work. The fresh buds are best, and these are gathered most often in the spring, occasionally in the winter. The tree itself is delicate and branches will break in heavy wind, this makes them easy to forage without damaging the tree itself. The young leaves and buds are made into a salve to procure pleasant dreams and prevent nightmares.

Ginkgo Biloba is sometimes called the Oldest tree in the world, a living fossil that has been around for over 200 million years. is a helpful herb if you have a hard time remembering your dreams. Many people say they dream much more when they take ginkgo. Ginkgo is an herb that helps with circulation. This works by increasing blood flow to the brain and elsewhere in the body. So maybe you are dreaming more when you take ginkgo, Or maybe you are remembering those dreams a little better. Because Ginkgo is a blood vessel dilator it can also help oxygenate the blood, allowing for better breathing. This herb can interfere with medications and is not recommended before surgery as it can thin the blood.

Star Anise is a fragrant and lovely spice often used in potpourris and as a flavoring in traditional Autumn foods. It is also known to help enhance psychic ability and relieve nightmares. This is a great addition to your formulas you may be using to enhance your powers of prophecy through dreaming. While it is not used for dreaming by itself, it is used in formulas to get messages from your dreams. The spice itself is warming and can help with circulation. Herbs with warming energy will help with the effectiveness of other herbs in the formula, allowing the capillaries to open up and for the other herbs to "catch a ride" on the circulatory effect. Topically it is also used as an antifungal remedy. Star anise is shown to contain shikimic acid which is an important ingredient in anti-influenza medications around the world. It takes a year to process and extract this compound from the star anise, and its price and availability will be affected by the demand for these influenza medications like Tamiflu. Note; Star anise and aniseed are two different plants.

Dream Revelation:

The following magical spell calls upon Hermes and Selene, both associated and conflated with the Goddess Hekate in the PGM.
You will need:
A Linen Strip
An Olive Branch
Hekates Ink

On the linen strip you will write your query in myrrh ink and wrap it in an olive branch and place it on the left side of your head. You will then go to sleep freshly bathed on a clean mat on the ground reciting the following spell seven times:

Recite:
"Hermes, lord of the world, who are in the heart,
O circle of Selene, spherical and square,
the founder of the words of speech,
pleaded of Justice's cause, garbed in a mantle,
with golden sandals, turning airy course beneath earth's depths,
who hold the spirit's reins,
the sun's and who with lamps of gods immortal give joy to those beneath earth's depths,
 to mortals who've finished life.
The Moirai's fatal thread and Dream divine
you're said to be, who send forth oracles by day and night;
 you cure the pains of all mortals with your healing care.
Hither, O blessed one, O mighty son
of the goddess who brings full mental powers,
by your own form and gracious mine.

And to an uncorrupted youth reveal a sign
and send him true your skill of prophecy,
    OIOSENMIGADŌN ORTHŌ BAUBŌ NIOĒRE
KODĒRETH DOSĒRE SYRE SUROE SANKISTĒ
DŌDEKAKISTĒ AKROUROBORE KODĒRE RINŌTON
KOUMETANA ROUBITHA NOUMILA PERPHEROU
AROUŌRĒR AROUĒR."

Try your best to say the Voces Magicae 7 times out loud.

The Voces Magicae are intended to have magic power, a type of language that is not easily translated nor possibly should be.

Olive

As you can see in the spell above, the Olive branch has also been associated with the Goddess Hekate. Porphyry Mentions "Her" Olive branch as being emblematic of her fiery nature in reference to the Goddess Hekate.

Olive Oil was held in High regard in Ancient Greece, it was used not only for food, but magically and medicinally as well. It would be used as an Anointing oil and it was applied on various parts of the body, as well as being an offering of supplication to the Gods. It was a symbol of Peace and Prosperity in ancient Rome and is still a symbol for this in modern Europe and the Modern Arab World.

More on Herbs

Sometimes herbs can silence the spirit of a person who has done harm, one might cut out the tongue of such a corpse and fill it with herbs used to encourage silence. In many cultures there is fear of the lingering dead, that they do not mean to help the living but they remain due to trauma or other unresolved issues. Herbs are used in the funerary process to mask smells, Preserve, protect, prevent disease and even to guide and help the spirit pass over.

In ancient Egypt many different herbs and resins were used to preserve the corpse itself. After the Body was dried out with Natron the following herbs used in the embalming process included Myrrh, Cinnamon, Saffron, Storax, Gum Mastic, Poppy, Cedar, Sandalwood and Rose. Many of these plants are mentioned in texts as herbs within the realm of Hekate.

Plants have been used to help guide the recently deceased or the restless dead and to help in the mourning process. Floral displays are commonly seen at funerals and planting certain trees or flowers on a grave is common practice we see in modern cemeteries today. Here are a few plants and how they are used.

Aconite *Aconitum Napellus* is sometimes called monkshood, wolfsbane, trolls hat, Queen of poisons, or devil's herb. It is said the Aconite was born of the saliva of Cerberus, The Three headed hound of Hekate, and this plant grows plentifully in her garden. Many witches use this toxic plant for protection and it was known to be one of the most poisonous plants in ancient Greece. The juice of the plant was used to tip arrows to hunt wolves, and this is where the name "Wolfs-Bane" originated.

Saffron *Crocus Sativus* Saffron is considered one of the most expensive spices in the world since it takes great care to harvest. There are often recommended substitutions because of the price of saffron itself. These Substitutions are typically calendula and safflower, but they are not exactly the same. "The Saffron Robed Queen"or "krokopeplos" is an epithet to Hekate which suggests it was used as dye in religious garments. Saffron was also used in perfumes and floral waters to draw in love, but it was also used to bathe the dead. Medicinally there are compounds in the Crocus Sativus that are found to help with depression as studies have shown it can modulate certain chemicals in the brain, including serotonin.

Sidr leaves *Ziziphus spina-christi*
In Islam these leaves are multi purpose, they can remove so called "black magic" and are used to wash the dead. These leaves have the added benefit of saponification, meaning they act like a soap when agitated in water.

"Take seven leaves of a green Sidr, grind them with two rocks, add water to it, read the verse of Al-Kursi and Al-Qawakil, take three sips, then wash up with the rest. This will remove all of his afflictions." (Curses, evil eye etc) Fath Al-Bari -10/233

One of the methods of bathing a corpse ~ "It is obligatory to bathe a dead body thrice. The first bath should be with water mixed with "Sidr" leaves. The second bath should be with water mixed with camphor and the third should be with clean water." … This type of ritual is traditionally practiced by people who are of the Islamic faith. From Articles of Islamic Acts.

Blackberry *Rubus armeniacus* it is said that blackberry can be planted on a grave to protect it from errant spirits. As a Hedge plant it is one that is used for protection of boundaries both spiritual and physical. When harvesting blackberries it is noted that they will often take their sacrifice in the way of blood for allowing you to harvest from them. The thorns on the plant indicate their protective and bloodthirsty nature. Their long tendrils of thorny branches find their way into the earth, often spreading fast and far.

It is said that when the devil was cast out of heaven, he fell on the blackberry bush, and when he did he pissed all over it, ruining the berries for the rest of the season. The thorns can be used in protective and baneful magic, the berries before October 11th can be used in workings of love and attraction as ink or edible potions. After October 11th blackberries can be used to make devils ink, when wishing to make pacts and/or create sigils in the ink.

Medicinally you can make a tea from the dried leaves of the plant that will help strengthen and tone the uterine muscles. Blackberry leaf is an astringent antibacterial that can also help as a mouthwash for gums and a sore throat. The large and beautiful roots can be made into a very strong antidiarrhetic tincture or tea.

Bay Laurel *Laurus nobilis* is a plant growing in Hekates Garden as described in the argonautica. Laurel is a symbol of victory and is used to create crowns to honor these victories. Bay leaves are a wonderful offering for your altar to the Gods. Bay Laurel is used for inducing visions, and manifestation works. Laurel was said to be burned in the Temples of Apollo in Delphi (The Oracle of Delphi) to help the oracles and induce prophetic Visions. It is native to the Mediterranean and typically associated with the sun god Apollo since his love interest was Daphne. Daphne rejected all advances to her and prayed to be rescued from all these suitors and so her father turned her into a Laurel. Laurels were made into wreaths placed on the body to invoke the blessings of the sun god Apollo. Many modern witches choose to write their desires onto the leaves, and place them into a cauldron of manifestation. Medicinally it is used to help with digestion, respiration and can soothe urinary tract infections. The leaves are added to stews and soups to help with digestion and to act as a carminative.

Belladonna *Atropa Belladonna*

Atropos was one of the three fates and She determined how a person would die and cut the cord of life. She was known as the unbendable one, as mortals are all connected through life and death and this is the unchanging fact of our existence. The attributes of Hekate and the fates play similar roles in Greek Mythology, as the ones who hold the key (or thread) of life, death and rebirth. A plant having a name associated with the fate who cuts the cord of Death should tell you how poisonous this plant is, but Belladonna it was used to dilate the eyes of women in times past, as it was said at the time to make a woman more beautiful. So it should be said that Belladonna is symbolic of a dangerous beauty, one that attracts and can kill if handled poorly.

Mullein: sometimes is considered a substitution for graveyard dirt (Though dubious) mullein has an association with the dead, illuminating pathways and revealing the truth about a situation.. The seed stalks can be made into torches by covering them in wax or lard. This is another hedge plant, one that grows on borders and crossroads, associated with Saturn due to it being an herb of boundaries both physical and spiritual.

Calendula *Calendula Officinalis :* an uplifting plant with affinity for the sun and fire. This herb can be used topically to ease redness and inflammation. Magically it is an herb of prosperity and sustainment of that prosperity. Calendula is also used in formulas to enhance psychic powers and is sometimes used as a substitute for the more expensive saffron crocus sativus.

Dandelion: *Taraxicum* Dandelion is a tonic for the liver and gallbladder as it can help excrete bile, making digestion an easier process. Magically it resembles one of Hekates' lit torches while maintaining its long taproot deep in the Earth and the chthonic realm. Old folk magic tells us that you can make a wish by blowing off every seed in one breath.

Mandrake *Mandragora genus* Acquiring a true mandrake root can be somewhat of a challenge, combine that with the fact that many ancient sources say it will only be an effective mandrake if it is harvested where the blood and/or semen of a murdered man had fallen. In the excerpt from *Argonautica* Below "Titans Root" came from an area of earth bathed in the Ichor (regurgitated Liver) of the Titan God Prometheus. Depending on what has nourished the Mandrake, the effects of such a plant will be noticed differently. It is implied that the mandrake root itself will take on the qualities of the person (or deity) from whom it takes its nourishment and will be especially powerful when calling on many epithets of Hekate. Here is the description~

Apollonius Rhodius, Argonautica 3. 840 ff :

"Medea wished to drive to the splendid Temple of Hekate; and while the handmaidens were getting the carriage ready she took a magic ointment from her box. This salve was named after Prometheus. A man had only to smear it on his body, after propitiating the only-begotten Maiden (*Koure mounogenes*) [Hekate] with a midnight offering, to become invulnerable by sword or fire and for that day to surpass himself in strength and daring. It first appeared in a plant that sprang from the blood-like ichor of Prometheus in his torment, which the flesh-eating eagle had dropped on the spurs of Kaukasos (Caucasus) . . . To make the ointment, Medea, clothed in black, in the gloom of night, had drawn off this juice in a Caspian shell after bathing in seven perennial streams and calling seven times on Brimo [Hekate], nurse of youth (*kourotrophos*), Brimo, night-wanderer of the underworld (*nyktipolis khthonie*), Queen of the dead (*anassa eneroi*). The dark earth shook and trembled underneath the Titan root when it was cut, and Prometheus himself groaned in the anguish of his soul."

Titan root, the plant that sprung from the "blood like ichor of prometheus" is Mandrake root.

You are encouraged to find your own mandrake and/or grow from seed. Working with this plant can take patience and time, so don't expect to be an expert at it right away. Dried mandrake roots can sometimes be acquired online for use, but do not use the substitute of mayapple. If you see Mandrake root being offered very cheaply and it does not say Mandragora Officionarum or Mandragora Autumnalis, it is not true mandrake.

Myrtle Myrtle is a fragrant plant most often associated with works of love and rebirth. In the PGM there is a spell to call upon the Goddess Hekate and the souls of the restless dead, to help gain the affection of a lover. Though this spell is coercive and does not sound like it would produce a very healthy relationship, It is meant to disrupt and antagonize the life of the intended target until they do what is desired by the practitioner. Here is an excerpt from the portion that talks about Myrtlewood being used in the coffin . It is an interesting use of a plant most associated with love and desire to coerce an individual into a relationship by also calling on the souls of unlucky heroes and luckless heroines.

"...Who rouses up with the fire Souls of the dead
Unlucky heroes. Luckless heroines.
Who in this place who on this day,
who in this hour, who, in coffins of **myrtlewood**,
 give heed to me and rouse her/NN.
On this night.and from her eyes remove sweet sleep
 Cause for her wretched care and fearful pain
 cause her to follow after my footsteps
 and / for my will give her a willingness
 until she does what i command of her
 oh mistress Hekate..."
PGM Betz. Page 68 (1419-1432)

Yew *Taxus Baccata* Is a tree found in many a cemetery and has been associated with death for thousands of years. Yew is commonly planted in graveyards and is thought to feed off the corpse, wrapping roots around the bones. When planted in the graveyard it is said to consume the body's vapors, and a corpse can be washed in a decoction of Yew. It has also been used for suicide and murder, as well, since the seeds are poisonous. Even in small amounts it will certainly cause death. Interestingly Yew trees are known to live a very long time, with its oldest tree in Europe being the Fortingall Yew estimated between 2,000 to 3,000 years old.

Poppy Flowers and seeds *papaver somniferum* This is the common breadseed poppy and there are many other variations of it as well. These flowers are placed into coffins or around the body to keep the dead asleep and to keep them from telling their secrets to the living. The Most famous use of poppy is it being the source of opium and that the seed pods of the plant contain thousands of nutritious seeds. The Seed Pods of Poppy symbolize plentitude and fertility. Hekate herself is pictured holding a poppy seed head in ancient artwork and the black poppy is also mentioned in the Argonautica as growing in her garden.

On Hekate: "Wherefore her power appears in three forms, having as symbol of the new moon the figure in the white robe and golden sandals, and torches lighted: the basket, which she bears when she has mounted high, is the symbol of the cultivation of the crops, which she makes to grow up according to the increase of her light: and again the symbol of the full moon is the goddess of the brazen sandals. Or even from her branch of olive one might infer her fiery nature, and from the poppy her productiveness, and the multitude of the souls who find an abode in her as in a city, for the poppy is an emblem of a city. " ~ Porphyry

Roses: A flower that is known for its beauty and fragrance is often used to symbolize love because of these qualities. It should also be noted that just as the rose is symbolic of beauty but it has a protective aspect to it as well. The thorns on the rose will draw blood if a person chooses to pluck the rose without consideration and care. You cannot simply grab a rose from the plant without first noting the thorns. Roses have the quality of giving you a lesson in Good Judgment, once you have carelessly grabbed a rose once, you will think twice about doing it again. That said they are common offerings left on graves reminding us all of the shared experience of life and death. Beauty and Pain are partners in this experience.

Cypress *Cupressus semperviren* A tree associated with Hekate and often found in cemeteries as it was symbolic of death and the underworld. Different varieties of Cypress can be found all over the world, and they all have similar energy. You can gather the resin from the trees, or use the leaves to create infused oil. It is said these resins can be used to dress a body in death and in Sapphos Conjectures it is mentioned

> "While Sappho's brows with cypress wreaths are drest
> Let one kind word my weary woes repay,
> Or, in eternal slumbers bid them rest."

Indicating it is a plant associated with Mourning.
It is said that Artemis was born in a grove of Cypress.

Wormwood *Artemisia Absinthium*

As a vermifuge, this relative of wormwood is used to expel parasites from the body and its medicinal action will tell you a lot about its magical action. Used in magical ink it will prevent papers from being destroyed by insects. It is used to help protect by repelling evil spirits and sorcery done against you. This bitter herb was symbolic of the grieving process and was burned as incense to honor the dead. Bags stuffed with wormwood are placed on cemetery gates to shield against evil spirits entering the cemetery. Wormwood is used in the popular drink Absinthe, and was used to increase psychic powers and summon the spirits of the dead. Porphyry, a devotee of the Goddess Hekate described how statuary should be decorated and suggested Hekate be decorated with branches of Wormwood. In the Greek Magical Papyri, Wormwood is used throughout, for various magic spells involving many Goddesses and Gods, including Hekate.

Rue *Ruta Graveolens*

Is known as the "Herb of Grace"

Rue is a powerful herb of Hekate and is used to consecrate tools of iron, it will help increase psychic powers and reverse the evil eye and send evil back from where it came. Rue water or a rue infusion can be sprinkled around the house with a sprig of Rosemary to help keep unwanted energy out. Rue is mentioned in Praeperaratio Evangelica as one of the ingredients to call on the Goddess Hekate to visit in your dreams. (See the Crescent Moon Journey). While rue is a plant that grows best in full sun, it is said to be best harvested at night due to the volatile oils. When these oils make contact with your skin and the sun's light touches it, it can cause a skin reaction much like poison oak to some people. If you harvest a small amount, or harvest at night this is usually not a problem.

Asphodel *Asphodelus genus*

As a plant of the crossroads of death and the underworld, the torch-like appearance of such a striking flower may inspire a spirit to be called into its light. The Asphodel itself is a flower of the crossroads or of the liminal space between decisions. It is mentioned as being a plant in Hekate's garden, from the orphic Argonautica, and you see Persephone to be Queen of the underworld who is crowned in asphodel.

"The ancients planted the (asphodel) flowers near tombs, regarding them as the form of food preferred by the dead, and many poems refer to this custom. The name is derived from a Greek word meaning scepter." (*Grieves a Modern Herbal) When someone carried a scepter it signified their power, or importance to a community in ancient Greece, Egypt and Mesopotamia.

This floral water of Asphodel is used to wash the corpse after death, and is helpful in easing the transition from one realm to another in this way, in addition to planting or placing the flowers on a grave.

The Asphodel Fields are mentioned in The Odyssey as being the place where ordinary souls went after death. After drinking from the river Lethe, and forgetting their former lives, they wandered the afterlife amidst the fields of asphodel. In some translations, it should be noted that there may be some discrepancy in that it could have been translated as "ash filled meadow" which should be a reminder to use your own best judgment when working with plants.

Of course this Greek myth can be relative to the era and the person telling the story. The underworld was not always translated in a consistent way, and even in modern times we see new stories being told of the afterlife, even in Greek mythology. It is interesting that there is a Greek saying, "He has forgotten his Asphodel" Which means he has forgotten where he came from.

The light scent of the flower itself helped when mourning a loved one. Would the scent invoke that feeling of déjà vu? Would it be something that can access this part of the underworld itself due to its relationship with its own fields and being the food of the dead? When using Asphodel, having the flowers with you during rituals involving summoning the dead can help bring messages from those who have passed on. If you do not have the fresh flowers available, you can imbibe asphodel honey. A spoonful by mouth of Asphodel Honey is best to taste the flowers in the sweet nectar of the bees work. It makes a suitable offering to the Goddess Hekate and her wandering souls as well. Other ways of using these flowers is to consecrate a wand or scepter with the waters of asphodel as this plant has associations with the wands in the tarot.

Garlic

Garlic and alliums in general were used throughout history to protect and expel evil from a location. Hanging a leek from the doorway was said to attract any disease to it and it would go to the leek and not the people in the home. Offerings of a wreath of Garlic at a crossroad to Hekate were a common practice in ancient Greece. Still to this day she is given garlic as an act of devotion and one that may protect the devotee from disease and the stings of scorpions.

Four Thieves Vinegar Recipe:

Combine the following fresh plants in equal parts to vinegar of choice. Wine vinegar is traditional, but any good strong vinegar will do.

Crushed Garlic
Rosemary
Thyme
Sage
Vinegar of choice

Use 1 part herbs, to two parts vinegar. Let infuse for one moon cycle and then strain.

This recipe is famously known for keeping grave robbers and thieves from becoming sick with the plague that killed their victims during the times of the Black Death.

There are some four thieves' vinegar recipes that are not meant to be ingested but this can be used to protect an area, or ingested to promote health when added to a glass of water or used on food. An area can also be sprinkled with the infused vinegar to protect an area. Helpful when you are having a ritual in a public space.

Lemon Herb Cake for Hekate Phosphoros:

Lemon is a useful ingredient to help clear confusion and it is reminiscent of light. Saffron, Calendula and dandelion all hold the power of the light of Hecate's Torches. This cake is a wonderful offering, but also one that can uplift and empower the ones who enjoy it.

1 ½ cups all-purpose flour
2 teaspoons baking powder
1 teaspoon salt
1 teaspoon ground saffron
2 lemons
1 cup white sugar
¼ cup white sugar
¾ cup lebne or Greek yogurt
2 duck eggs
½ cup butter/ melted
Handful of yellow dandelion flower petals
Handful of calendula flowers garbled

1. Heat oven to 350 degrees
   Grease a round 9 inch pan (measurement across entire the pan)
2. Whisk the one and a half cup of flour, the two teaspoons of baking powder, one teaspoon saffron powder, one teaspoon of salt together in a large bowl
3. Grate the Zest from the lemons and place in a small bowl mixed with the cup of white sugar. Half a lemon and squeeze out the lemon juice into another small bowl.

4. Cut the remaining zested lemons into thin rounds and place in a frying pan with a ¼ cup sugar and let cook on low heat to make candied lemon peels and lemon syrup.

5. Whisk in the ¾ cup lebne or yogurt, 2 eggs and lemon juice to the wet mixture of lemon juice.

6. Add the wet mixture to the flour mixture and stir to blend. Add the half cup of melted butter. Add your calendula petals and dandelion petals. Pour the batter into your round pan. Place your candied lemon on the top with the syrup evenly over the batter. Place in the oven and cook for 55 minutes or until golden brown. Let cool.

Herbal Actions and Properties

Here are some useful terms in regard to the herbal path.

Abortifacient – Something that will induce abortion.

Adaptive – Strengthens the immune system and helps the body to deal with stress.

Alterative – Nourishes and tonifies the body. Helps to process metabolic waste.

Analgesic – Helps to relieve or reduce pain.

Anaphrodisiac – will decrease sexual desire

Anesthetic – will induce the loss of sensation or consciousness due to the depression of nerve function

Antibacterial – stops the growth of bacteria

Anticatarrh – reduces inflamed mucous membranes

Antidepressant – acts to alleviate mental depression

Antidiabetic – prevents or relieves diabetes

Antidiarrhetic –prevents or treats diarrhea

Antiemetic – stops vomiting

Antifungal – inhibits the growth of fungus

Antihemorrhagic – controls hemorrhaging or bleeding

Anti-infectious – counteracts infection

Anti-inflammatory – controls inflammation

Antimicrobial – destroys microbes

Antioxidant – inhibits oxidation

Antipruritic – can relieve itching

Antipyretic – reduces fever

Antirheumatic – eases pain of rheumatism and inflammation of joints and muscles

Antiseptic – something that will reduce the possibility of infection.

Antispasmodic – calms nervous and muscular spasms.

Antitussive – prevents cough

Antiviral – impairs virus

Aphrodisiac –Helps to increase sexual desire

Aromatic – a fragrant herb or plant that offers healing potential

Astringent – constricts and binds by coagulation of proteins

Bitter – stimulates digestive function

Bronchial –relaxes spasms or constriction of the lungs

Carcinostatic –inhibits the development or continued growth of cancer

Cardiotonic – increases strength and tone of the heart

Carminative -- causes the release of gas

Catarrhal – inflammation of mucous membranes of the head and throat with excessive discharge of mucus.

Caustic – contains acidic compounds that have a corrosive action that is capable of burning or eating away living tissues

Cholagogue – increases flow of bile

Counterirritant – a substance which creates irritation or mild inflammation in one location with the goal of lessening discomfort and/or inflammation in another location.

Demulcent – soothes and protects inflamed and irritated mucous membranes both topically and internally

Dermatitis – inflammation of the skin

Diaphoretic – increases perspiration

Digestive – aids the digestion process

Disinfectant – destroys pathogenic microbes

Diuretic – increases urine flow

Emetic – Induces vomiting

Emmenagogue – regulates menstruation

Emollient – softens the skin

Errhine –stimulates sneezing, increasing flow of mucus in nasal passages

Estrogenic – causes the production of estrogen

Euphoriant – produces a sense of bodily comfort

Expectorant – facilitates removal of mucus

Febrifuge – reduces or relieves fever

Galactagogue – promotes the flow of milk

Hemagogue – promotes the flow of blood

Hemostatic – controls or stops the flow of blood

Hepatic – having to do with the liver

Herpetic – treats skin eruptions relating to herpes

Hypertensive – raises blood pressure

Hypnotic – strong-acting nervous system relaxant (nervines) supports healthy sleep

Hypoglycemant – lowers blood sugar

Hypotensive – lowers blood pressure

Lactifuge – reduces the flow of milk

Laxative – loosens bowel contents, something to treat constipation

Lithotriptic – a substance that causes kidney or bladder stones to dissolve

Masticatory – increases flow of saliva upon chewing

Mucilaginous – polysaccharide-rich compounds that soothe inflamed mucous membranes

Narcotic – induces sleep, or stupor, and lessons pain

Nephritic – something that has a beneficial influence on the kidneys

Nervine – a nerve soothing herb

Nootropic – improves cognitive function, memory and mood, reduces oxidative damage to the brain

Nutritive – an herb containing nutrients

Refrigerant – an herb or a substance that cools the body

Relaxant – tends to relax and relieve muscular tension

Renal –strengthens or treats imbalanced issues affecting the kidneys

Rubefacient – reddens and dilates the blood vessels. Increases blood supply locally

Sedative – exerts a soothing and calming effect on the body

Soporific -- induces sleep

Stimulant – increases body or organ function temporarily

Stomachic – aids the stomach and digestive action

Sudorific – increase perspiration (sweating)

Tonic – stimulates energy and increases strength and tone

Vermifuge – expels worms

Vulnerary – aids in healing wounds

Sources:
Theoi.com
"Master Book of Herbalism" by Paul Beyerl
"Occult Botany" by Paul Sedir
"The Odyssey" Translation by Patrick Dunn
"Homer's Asphodel Meadow" Steve Reece
"A Modern Herbal" by Margaret Grieves
"Orphic Argonautica" Apollonius Rhodius
"Sleep Paralysis
A guide to Hypnagogic Visions & Visitors of the Night"
By Ryan Hurd
"Under the Witching Tree" by Corinne Boyer
"The Witches Cabinet" by Corinne Boyer
"Bibliotheca Valenciana" José Leitão
"Circle of Hekate" by Sorita Deste
"The Witching Herbs" by Harold Roth
"Myths and Legends of Flowers" by Charles M. Skinner
"Invasive Plant Medicine" by Timothy Lee Scott
"Hekate Soteira" Sarah Iles Johnson
"Plants of Life, Plants of Death" Frederick J. Simoons
"The Greek Magical Papyri in Translation" Hans Dieter Betz
www.hekatecovenant.com
"Magic Witchcraft and Ghosts in the Greek and Roman Worlds"
Daniel Ogden
"The Discovery of Witchcraft" Reginald Scot
"The Sacred Herbs of Samhain" Ellen Evert Hopman

Other Books by Jennifer Teixeira include:

"Sorceress of Angra"

&

"Temple of the Bones"